Once
Round
the
Lump

Published & Printed by Pickard Communication,
10-11 Riverside Park, Sheaf Gardens, Sheffield S2 4BB
Telephone 0114 275 7222
www.pickardcommunication.co.uk

CONTENTS

I dedicate this book to the memory of
my hard working parents George and Jennie Sapcote.
I pray God's Eternal Peace & Blessings on their Souls.

Preface

Blue Remembered Hill Top

I always thought my childhood was a figment of my imagination because there is nothing left of the homes and streets I grew up in. I could never say to my grandchildren, "Look, this is the house where I was born" or "These are the streets where I played", because apart from a small collection of family photographs, I have nothing but my memories. What a joy it was then to open up two recent publications by an old neighbour, which were packed full of photos of long forgotten friends, the streets we played on, the firms we worked for and the shops we spent most of Saturday in.

There have been many books published on the subject of the old township of Attercliffe – everything from the Neolithic to the Victorian and as I have always believed history should be about people and not princes, I think the time is right to start sharing memories and photographs while we are still around. It will be good for our grandchildren to know about the sort of lives we led before the advent of "the blessed box", or what we did to occupy ourselves from dawn till dusk without getting under our mother's feet and without needing a wage packet to fund it. But if we are to get a real view of how life was in the mid twentieth century through to its demise, then who can describe it better than those who lived and worked in that very district that still holds our minds and hearts, even though we were all moved out a quarter of a century ago in some mad Latter Day Clearances.

Our surroundings may have looked grim on the surface but a closer examination would have revealed a community that was vibrant and exiting. There was a culture of full employment and youngsters had lots to do after school. The facilities we had were second to none: play-centres, youth clubs, churches, chapels and all the clubs attached to them. We had cinemas, pubs, sports clubs, a library, a park, a swimming pool, dance halls, snooker halls, and the money to go to them.

Heritage is tradition repackaged as the spectacular *

Men and women worked hard in the forges, mines and mills of the East End and produced the materials and rolling stock that moved the world – so much so, that we can say with all honesty that this country's greatness and success was due to their labours and that the present generation is indeed *standing on the shoulders of giants*. **Those giants were our parents and grandparents. The sacrifices they made at the point of production, where every week they were 'robbed blind ageyen' as my dad used to say when opening his wage packet and in the effect hard labour and working conditions had on their health, and in bringing up families in conditions beyond the comprehension of today's 20 somethings, were astonishing.

Today the lives and times of 19th and 20th century working people are seen as something both to wonder at and to pity. What was the norm and everyday is now viewed as something dramatic that should be displayed in a museum. Ironically this is the mainstay of much of today's recreation economy. But for those of us who were there, it was the best of times in terms of social cohesiveness, of knowing who we were, and living in harmony with our neighbours and surroundings.

Every age must be successful in whatever it does so that it may pass on the baton of commercial success to the next generation; that is why things had to change. But at what cost? "Throwing the baby out with the bathwater" is a saying that springs to mind when I think about what happened to our community and for a full thirty years the land was left derelict and renamed the 'Attercliffe Environmental Corridor'. I ask you, what was that all about? Yes, we needed new homes but we could have been re-housed street by street and our community could have continued.

As a local history student I became more and more interested in the type and condition of the houses we lived in, how much rents we paid and to whom and so on and I hope you find this as absorbing as I have. It is also a history of that part of Attercliffe called Hill Top and Carbrook, of the bustling, chaotic and hilarious lives of its inhabitants and more important, of our place in its history, of the homes we grew up in and street we played in, where after being called in at dusk we were always allowed one more run around the lump before going to bed.

Ann Sapcote

*Professor Giddings Chancellor of the London School of Economics in his 1999 Radio 4 Reith Lectures
**Sir Isaac Newton in a Letter to the philosopher and scientist Robert Hooke, 1676. "If I have seen further, it is by standing on the shoulders of giants", also seen on the rim of the two-pound coin.

On the Common c.1800

The Common at Carbrook before the Enclosure Act. Note the body of Spence Broughton on the gibbet.

The Law doth punish man or woman,

Who steals the goose from off the common.

But lets the greater felon loose,

Who steals the land from off the goose!

From Rural Village to Industrial Township

Attercliffe, as we learned at school, was a Saxon hamlet and had been recorded in The Doomsday Book. Much of our history may be gleaned from old church documents so it is from the *Survey of the Parish of Sheffield: the Township of Attercliffe-cum-Darnall* we learn that in 1649 the Parliamentary Commissioners, being concerned with the growing population in Attercliffe Village and the surrounding districts of Darnall, Carbrook, parts of Grimesthorpe and Brightside and their need to conduct their own sacraments, baptisms, marriages, churching of women and burials, state:

> The chappellrye consists of about two hundred and fiftye
> famelyes. Therefore wee thinke fitt that the said chappell
> of Attercliffe to be made a parish church:"

The Parliamentry Returns for 1649

I use the term Attercliffe Village to cover the area between Washford Bridge and Kirkbridge Road because to go beyond the Kirkbridge Dyke was to go on to The Common and the districts of Hill Top and Carbrook. The earliest information about Attercliffe I have come across is concerning the wills of some local people who lived in Attercliffe Village in 15th and 16th Centuries. Between Zion Lane and the old course of the Don was the area known as The Dick Bank. This was a small copse and enclosed meadow and orchard. In the 1700s it was known as Kay's Meadow. Elizabeth Rhodes' house at Washford Bridge was built with stone taken from the Dick Bank, and records in Sheffield Archives show surveys and costings made by the surveyor Fairbank in the 1790s with regards to repairing the wall around the orchards. Apparently nicking stone from the Dick Bank was a problem since records were kept!

The Dick Bank has a long history, and in this first case sample, it is mentioned in the will and estate of one Thomas Grayson of Grymethorpe. The Will was written in English, an important development as legal documents were usually written in Latin. Perhaps this was a sign of the growing confidence local people had about themselves and their place in the community.

1564 Will (in English) of Thomas Grayson of Grymethorpe…..Testator gave to John Swynden and Agnes his wife'…….my whole yeares of my farme which I now dwell on, with a close at Attercliffe called Dickbanke butting up Hawkeffur;' to Eliz. his daughtr….' thre kye gates in the aforesaid close duringe my years paying the halfe rent to John Swynden and Agnes his wife during the said lease;' to his brother John his….' best jacket and his best dublet; his best hoise, a velvet nyght cap and vis.viid. in money'

1430 The Vigil of Saint Lawrence (9th August) The will (in Latin) of William Byrley of Attercliffe butcher (flesshewer)…..to the High Altar for forgotten tithes 6s. 8d.; to the fabric of the chancel of Saint Crux 20s.; to the vicar 12d.; to every priest 10d.; to the clerks present at his funeral 3s 1d.; to be bestowed upon the poor 40s.; for buying victuals for the poor on the day of his burial, and the eighth day after £4.

1545 The will (in English) of John Birley of Attercliffe yeoman, directed that he should be buried in the churchyard of Sheffield. Testator gave to Hugh Swan his 'Bellowes, sithes, hamors and tonges' with all things belonging to the smythe; to the said Hugh, 'the horse whele and harnes'; to the wife of Edward Hyley, 'one cowe or 20s.'

1549 In the third year of Edward VI. The will (in English) of John Nodder of Attercliffe in the parish of Sheffield 'hardwareman', directed that he should be buried in the churchyard of Sheffield and for his mortuary according to the King's Acts. Testator gave to his 'moder' 44s.; to his 'broder' Thomas his 'best rayment viz: jackett, dublet, hoise, sherte, bonett, shois'…..

1563 Will (in English) of Catherine Carre of Attercliff. Amongst other legacies of cattle sheep and clothing given to her children, she gave them to Heughe, Katherine and Margaret, all her 'woll that is in the house to make them close'; and to Margaret her best kirtle; to Ellenor her sister, ' a redd kirtle'; to her children, 'the troughe of my whele during all my terme that is to spend savinge the last year and Roger my sone to have the oversight of the said whele trough during the said years for the children's profett and the last year to have it in his owne handes for his paynes takynge.'

Extract from ' A Catalogue of the Ancient Charter belonging to the Twelve Capital Burgesses and Commonality of the Town and Parish of Sheffield' Compiled by T.Walter Hall

Between that period in our history and the time I spent at Attercliffe (1947-1971) was more than a little hazy. However, after a very interesting course I attended at the W.E.A. in the old Attercliffe Vicarage, a clearer picture emerged. I had assumed that everything I'd seen or known as a child growing up in my beloved Attercliffe had always been there. In terms of family links we had been there a very long time. One of my ancestors, John Toes, had his birth registered at Attercliffe in 1811 and his father's occupation was recorded as flax grower and Excise man. Our more immediate ancestors, The Millers, were spring knife makers and publicans who ran The Cutlers Arms and The Travellers Inn in the 1860s are well documented by Vine in his definitive book on our township: The Story of Old Attercliffe, who says the Miller family came to Attercliffe in the late 1700s and according to his research one Miller was registered as apprentice to a master cutler: Richard Swallow in the 1690s.

Our streets, homes and places of work in the zenith of the Industrial Age gave an impression of permanency and history but in fact they had only been there for about a hundred and fifty years. Why did Attercliffe expand at the rate it did? Why were so many works located in one relatively small area? Why were street upon street of new homes built and why were men and women coming to Attercliffe in their thousands? Answer: to take up work in the newly built steelworks. And why were so many steelworks located in one area? The answer to that lies in the Enclosure Act of 1811, the building of the canal in 1819, the railways in the 1840's and the great steel-making discoveries of the 1860's that changed the world forever.

The Bessemer process allowed for mass production of steel and led to the great steelwork complexes that most of us worked for and lived next door to. An Act of Parliament made all this possible. Common lands were sold off and opened up for development. Also the fact that the east end of Sheffield was perhaps the only flat area where all the other variables came together was another extremely fortuitous coincidence. It was as if a spark of electricity had been applied to a primordial handful of mineral packed sludge that created the Big Bang that was Attercliffe! And this is where our history begins.

The Enclosure Act of 1811

The Enclosure Acts were first passed in Elizabethan times but increased at great pace between 1700 and 1800 because of the dramatic increase in the population of England and Wales. Though there was much hostility at the time it was in retrospect a good thing as it opened up and organized waste-land for economic expansion. The enclosing or taking in of waste-lands began to make a difference to the landscape in our region after the Act was passed. However, the landscape did not change over night and the Attercliffe we knew was still fifty years away. The poor who had lived on or near The Common for generations could no longer put their animals out to graze or collect kindling, and ancient pathways were lost. Poor farmers, who had worked and lived on common land for centuries but had nothing in writing to prove their rights, lost out to those who could. It was also noted that when the common land at Attercliffe was divided up it was given to those already well off, which led to many dissatisfied people taking to the streets and rioting. The anger felt by those whose loss was greatest was reflected in a popular verse of the time written by our old friend A Non.

> The Law doth punish man or woman,
> Who steals the goose from off the common.
> But lets the greater felon loose,
> Who steals the land from off the goose!

The Registry of Births in the Attercliffe Chapelry between 1720-1811 show fathers who came to baptise their children were mainly cutlers, colliers, scissor smiths and labourers. What type of labourers they were is not recorded, but as there were many farms still being worked up to the great housing boom of the 1860s, they could well have been farm labourers.

Minority employments registered were papermaking, silk weaving, collar making, stay making, one streetseter (road maker?), iron stone miners, a sprinkling of maltsters, victualers and one industry vital to every hearth: the frying pan maker! Other registrations of interest are: the baptism of Charles, son of Sarah and Captain John Chreighton in 1795, an officer in the army together with entries of soldiers who baptised their children at Hill Top in the late 1790's and early 1800's. Also the burial of the two week old child of John, a warfe carer and Emmelea Russell in 1811. The name Tinsley is written as a surname but as they appear to have two perhaps that was where they lived i.e. by the River Don wharf at Tinsley. Baptism records post 1811 show a steep rise in the number of colliers in Attercliffe. The getting of coal in our district has a very long history perhaps from Roman times and certainly well established before the year 1762 when Vine recorded the following:

> Wm Milner owner of the present Carltonville road (pit) and the
> adjacent part of the Recreation Ground had trouble in 1762
> arising from the transportation of his coals (5s 10d. per ton)
> across the common to the town.
>
> *(A History of Old Attercliffe, p283)*

The Great Land Grab.

The Plan of Awards relating to The Common at Attercliffe in 1811.

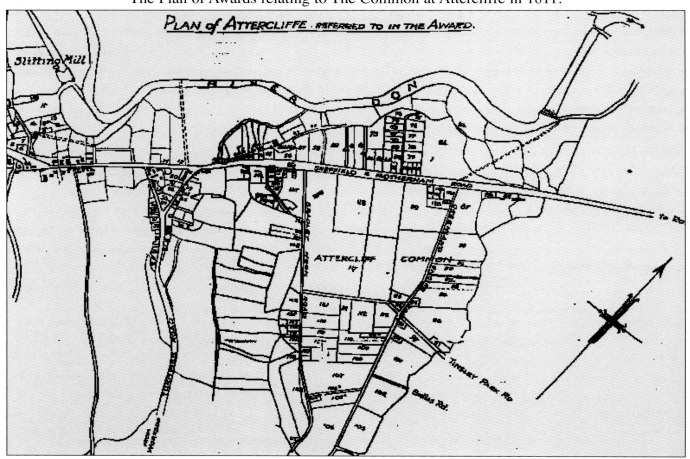

(provenance unknown)

The waste- land on the edge of our village was parcelled up for sale to property speculators and industrialists. In Carbrook, the Southeron family inherited the Bright Estates and held the land between Weedon Street and Milford Street. This was augmented by another ten acres by the Commissioners taking their southern boundary to Wentworth Lane. This may have been the Wentworth Road/Tuxford Road of our day. Lucy Southeron sold half of her estate in 1819 to Booth & Co. Iron Founders at Brightside. They later sold out to William Jessop around 1841.

The biggest tenant farmer in our district was George Bradford whose name we remember in Bradford Street. James Speed another tenant farmer whose 36-acre farm stretched over Rotherham and Steadfast Streets and other parts of the common was still, according to Vine in The Story of Old Attercliffe, working the land up to 1860.

The Duke of Norfolk came away with a handsome portion, for he got all the land between Coleridge Road and Broughton Lane up to that area we knew as Top Common. When the duke in turn sold off the land to developers and the canal builders the Enclosure Act allowed him the keep the rights to the coal under the soil. The canny duke happened to own that part of The Common where a dozen or so shafts were sunk and where the canal company planned to cut right through the middle. They actually cut through the High Hazels Seam, which it exposed by Cutty Meadows (Tinsley Park Road) and on the opposite bank. Vast amounts of coal had to be left for its own security. The mining companies operated the pits in Hill Top and Carbrook under licence from the Duke of Norfolk through the Sheffield Coal Company. In direct competition to him were the mines belonging to Earl Wentworth and William Staniforth of Tinsley Park and Darnall.

The Ordnance Survey Map of 1851 shows old coal pits at the bottom of Milford Street, at the junction of Carltonville Road with Attercliffe Common, on the Recreation ground boundary with the Co-op Garages and three pits by Broughton Lane Bridge. The Carbrook Colliery was at the rear of The Pheasant and other pits were on Bullas Lane and Bullas Road opposite Stovin Road. The Greenland Colliery was situated between Palmer Road and Coleford Road. The Chesterfield map of 1835 shows the line of a rail track running from a colliery at Handsworth through Darnall past the Greenland Colliery by Palmer Road and onwards on the line of the present Greenland Road ending at Attercliffe Common where the coal was loaded onto carts and transported to Sheffield and Rotherham. The name Greenland Engine Road refers to the Great Newcomen

Atmospheric Engine used to pump out the workings at the Greenland Colliery. The Darnall pits were as early as the 1700's supplying half of all households in Sheffield with domestic coal.

Some may remember Arthur Balfour's works by Bullas Road. Here were some allotments and behind them in the woods were some disused bell pit workings that had long been overgrown and half filled in. This was a popular place for the young lads of our day to show off their cycling skills by riding at top speed along the narrow paths between each of the pits. These were the snake paths and the old bell pits they ran the risk of falling into were the most primitive of workings in this district which had long been abandoned perhaps as early as the mid-eighteen hundreds. Though as with many of the old workings that were not economically viable, they still held sufficient amounts to be claimed by local people in times of need. Mainly slack and coal dust, briquettes could be made into the famous Jubilee of legend.

 Bradley Nook Road which later became Coleridge Road took its name from the Long and Short Bradley Fields that ran between Phillimore Road and Henson Street of our day. The Twelve Capital Burgesses owned this land and monies accrued by renting out the fields went to the Church. The two road names, Bradley Nook Road and Greenland Engine Road epitomised two diverse landscapes and the social and economic activities in our district at this period in its development and the Fairbank Brothers surveyed much of our district at this time and their maps and pocket sketches show in great detail every field, close and orchard. It could only have been in Attercliffe where such wholesome rural activities as milking cows and the washing of sheep in the lamb pool by Janson Street could co-exist alongside the filth of the Industrial Revolution.

Attercliffe Hill Top and The Windmill

As a child the only time I heard the name 'Hill Top' was when someone was going to Mr Hunt's dairy opposite Whitworth Lane to fetch ice cream. Yet whenever I open up a map of Attercliffe, there the name is as the official one for that area around the old chapel. I have also noted that on really old maps printed before 1880 the original name for Whitworth Lane was Hill Top Road, which carried on up through what eventually became Brown Bayley's scrap yard to the point where it met Milner Road. Both these roads were swallowed up in Brown Bayley's early expansions. I've always been puzzled by the name Hill Top as Attercliffe Village is on higher ground but further research found the answer in the "Survey of the Parish of Sheffield- The Township of Attercliffe cum Darnall." and refers to the area around the old chapel.

> 'The chapel is a modest building, placed on an
> eminence rising abruptly from the meadows
> near the Don........'   (ibid)

You see, I wasn't looking in the right place and a walk on the new path by the River Don between Newhall Bridge and Abyssinia Bridge shows its eastern bank significantly higher. If you study the bench-marks on the Ordnance Survey map of 1903 then you will see that the land gets even steeper at the Pothouse Bridge (Coleridge Road Bridge). Further down the river in the direction of Carbrook Weir, the original river-bank panned out into flat land with a steep rise butting up Milford Street and as our rivers were the original means of getting from one place to another in historic times then it makes sense to name areas as they were seen by river traffic. I would imagine the land was even higher in the days before the massive house building and road schemes altered the topography our district forever. Imagine if you will, great steam driven earth- movers flattening out the hillocks and waysides of the old common. The Hill Top Chapel or to give its proper name, 'The Chapel of Jesus Christ, Saviour' was

> '....placed at the very extremity of the village of Attercliffe
> that it might be near to the principal promoter of the work
> -Mr. Bright of Carbrook.'   (ibid.)

The Ordnance Survey map of 1851 records the Old Attercliffe Pottery which was roughly where Amberley Road met Edward Road with old pit shafts dotted around Carbrook that were once worked by the Sunderland Moor Colliery. The residence of it owner, Sunderland Lodge at the Pit Close was situated between Belmoor Road and Berkley Road. Belle Vue, on the site of Carbrook Recreation ground, was the home of John Terry one time publican of The Travellers further up Attercliffe. Also shown is Johnson Lane (Janson Street) which was also known as Lamb Pool Lane and referred to the place where shepherds took their flocks to be washed and lived on in the name of the pub which stood on its corner with Attercliffe Common for 120 years.

Attercliffe Old Pottery on Pothouse Lane (Coleridge Road) was actually established in the 1790's and owned by the family who also owned the wind-mill on Bold Street. The owners lived in Don Bank House, a substantial property at the side of the windmill that gave its name to Windmill Street across the river on the Newhall Estate. Being such a large house with its frontage facing the river and its back doors facing Bold Street, it seemed a little out of place when the new streets were set out in the 1860's. In the late 1950's Mrs Elsie Queen of Manningham Road moved here. Mrs Queen was a well known member of the community who owned the greengrocers shop at the top of Edward Road and was at the time the only woman in Sheffield to run a coaching business with her famous Queen of The Road charabancs. Mrs Queen began her business career by taking neighbours on day trips to the countryside and seaside. I have particular fond memories of these trips, Bakewell one day or Blackpool the next in the school holidays. These were very important to us, as our parents were unable to afford holidays in boarding houses. Mrs Queen's new home at Don Bank House on Bold Street was still there I believe when Attercliffe was cleared in the early 1970's.

It's hard to imagine our rural past given all the grime and noise of industrial Atttercliffe we were familiar with but rural it was and what better description can we have of Old Attercliffe than that from Ralph Skelton jnr writing in 1915. His father represented the people of Attercliffe-cum-Darnall as an elected member of the town council for fifteen years whose impressive memorial, looking like Cleopatra's Needle, may be seen in the old burial ground of Christ Church Attercliffe Road.

There was no prettier place for miles round than was Attercliffe fifty or sixty years ago: fine houses, Milner's, Huntsman's, Skelton's, the Vicarage, New Hall, Dr. Shaw's, all finely wooded, made a picture difficult to match. Pen and pocket- knife makers were busy in their little workshops, Coe and Lister, the Gascoignes, the Millers: women file cutters. The shops were small and country-like, the canal banks picturesque, the railway new, several farms, waiving crops – and many old cronies!"   *(Vine: The Story of Old Attercliffe. p.229)*

An artist's impression of the old windmill and Don Bank House as seen from the River Don.

'The old wind-mill property was unquestionably a rural feature of Hill Top a century or more ago; nestling around the mill with its great wind driven sails was the home of James Hill and family, along with the requisite farm and corm-mill buildings. The tall chimney bore the date 1832, showing that it was built when steam power was coming into vogue. Miller Hill's 12 acres of farm- land extended along the riverside a little beyond the end of modern Amberley Street, and correspondingly along the main road. Much of this had been enclosed from The Common by the Commissioners in 1811 and sold to Mr Hill for £306." *(ibid)*

Attercliffe Old Pottery – a little Potted History.

Vine recalls many pottery manufacturers working in this area between 1850-1870 at the Attercliffe Old Pottery. The Old Pottery covered the area where Freddie Thornhill had his yard and stables between Amberley Road and Edward Road right up to where the Rag Yard was. The clay pits which sourced the production, were further up Amberley Road, nearly to the top where it met Manningham Road. There used to be a selection of small pots and clay jars on shelves inside the Rag Yard on Edward Road kept as curios from the past, so presumably the production of domestic pottery was also one of their concerns. Their main one I would imagine, especially when the building work started, being the making of bricks and drain-pipes for the new houses that were going up. Let us see what Vine has to say about this in 'The Story of Old Attercliffe'.

'On the area out lined by Berkley, Coleridge and Manningham roads, owned by James Hill and son, were John Fearnley's Pottery Works early in the last century: in the 'fifties Richard Bedford was at work here in the 'Attercliffe Old Pottery': Thomas Steade in 1871-2 seems to have been last in the field. What a number of brick makers and earthenware manufacturers were active in Carbrook, Hill Top.......in those years.'

James Hill's son George advertised the pottery to let in the Leeds Mercury in 1844.

'....it is in complete working order, with a twelve month's stock of clay, prepared ready for use. The clay is got on the premises. The Oven holds 350 Dozen ware; is the only Coarse Ware Pottery (except one)* within twelve miles of Sheffield'

*This was the Attercliffe New Pottery on Worksop Road by Doctor Lane.

(Yorkshire Pots & Potteries: H. Lawrence)

The last potter, Thomas Steade, worked the site until 1871. Leaseholds for the new properties built on the site date from 1871. In 1890, when the leases went up for sale, the rents for the houses in this block that was situated between Edward Road and Pothouse Lane were 3/9 per week and according to the sale plans "were always let" as they were very near the Steelworks of Brown, Bayley's and Burrow's South Yorkshire Iron Works. The land was built upon piecemeal and completed around 1900. The O.S.Map of 1903/4 shows the area complete and the Directory for 1905 shows the name of Pothouse Road changed to Manningham Road.

This photograph taken by an employee at Brown Bayley's in the 1970's, shows what is obviously a building from a much earlier period than those surrounding it and was most likely part of the S. H. Burrows South Yorkshire Iron Works that stood on the corner of Coleridge and Manningham Roads, a company Brown Bayley's took over in 1928.

As part of the brickwork is whitewashed it was most likely enclosed by another building and forgotten about – thankfully – until further developments exposed it again. The roof was the red pan tile type with the remains of what looks like a chimneystack below the sky light. The curved top of the window opening would have housed a multi paned single opener contemporary with its period.

On some maps of the early 1830s, a building in the coal yard below the Pothouse Bridge Wharf is marked out but it may well have been part of the Old Pottery. We shall never know, but thanks to the enquiring eye of local historian H. Clayton (Technical Services dept.) who published it in the Brown Bayley Newsletter of 1972, we are that much wiser.

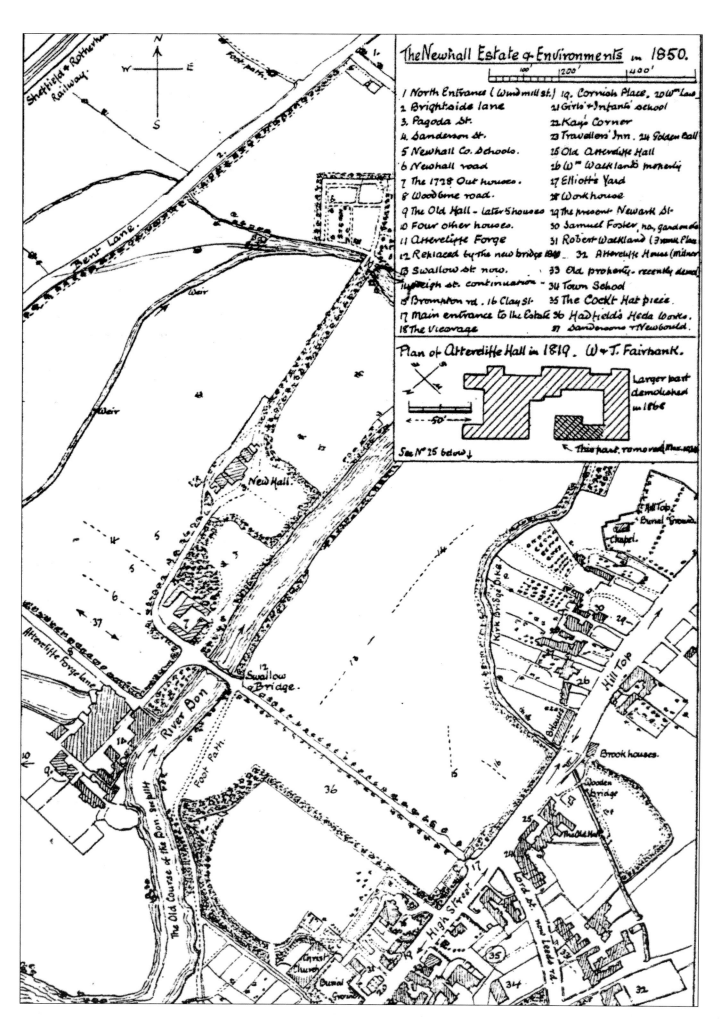

The Newhall Estate & Environments in 1850.

100'   200'   400'

1 North Entrance (Windmill St.)   19. Cornish Place, 20 Wm Lane
2 Brightside Lane   21 Girls' & Infants' school
3 Pagoda St.   22 Kay's Corner
4 Sanderson St.   23 Travellers' Inn. 24 Golden Ball
5 Newhall Co. Schools.   25 Old Attercliffe Hall
6 Newhall road   26 Wm Walkland's property
7 The 1728 Out houses.   27 Elliott's Yard
8 Woodbine road.   28 Workhouse
9 The Old Hall - later 5 houses   29 The present Newark St.
10 Four other houses.   30 Samuel Foster, no, garden &c
11 Attercliffe Forge   31 Robert Walkland (Front Place
12 Replaced by the new bridge 1849   32 Attercliffe House (Milner
13 Swallow St. now.   33 Old property, recently deml
14 Leigh st. continuation -   34 Town School
15 Brompton rd. 16 Clay St.   35 The COCKT Hat piece
17 Main entrance to the Estate   36 Hadfield's Steel works.
18 The Vicarage   37 Sandersons & Newbould

Plan of Attercliffe Hall in 1819. (W & T. Fairbank.

Larger part
demolished
in 1866

50'

See No 25 below ↓   ← This part, removed Mar. 1924

14

The Common in 1851

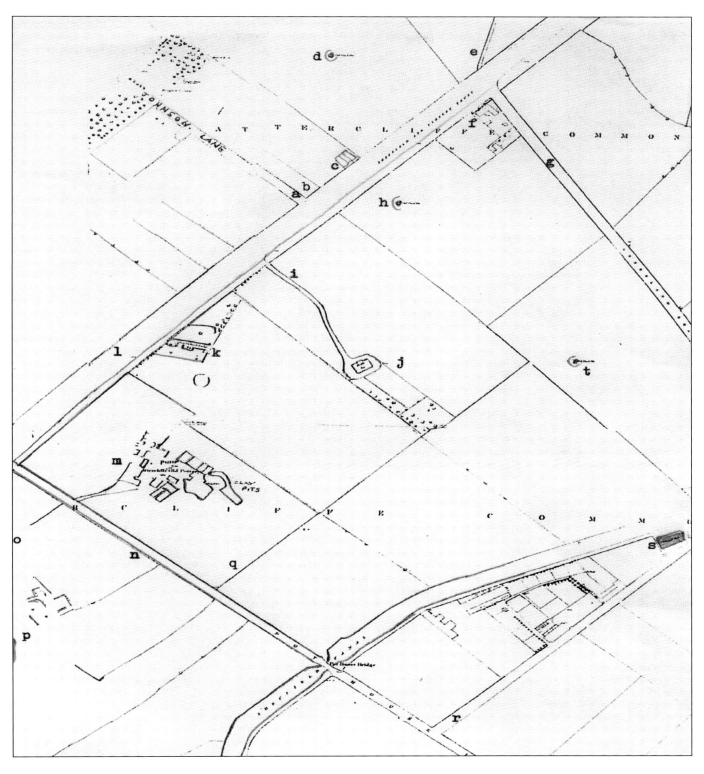

a Lambpool Lane/Johnson Lane/Janson Street   **b** site of Lambpool Hotel   **c** the new cottages   **d** old coal mine

e footpath to Carbrook Wier & Brightside Forge   **f** the Broughton buildings   **g** Greenland (Engine) Road

h old coal mine   **i** the original line of Terry Street   **j** Belle View House (in the rec)

k Sunderland Lodge at the Pit Close (between Berkley Road and Belmoor Road)

l Sheffield & Tinsley Trust Road/ Attercliffe Common   **m** Attercliffe Old Pottery

n BradleyNook Road/Pot House Lane/ Coleridge Road

o land belonging to Samuel Glave. **p** farm buildings and pond on Hill Top Road/Whitworth Lane

q line of PothouseRoad/Manningham Road   **r** Tinsley Park Road   **s** Canal Side cottages   **t** old coal mine.

Only the new cottages and Canal Side Cottages were still there in the 1950/60's

The Attercliffe Collieries.

*Rev. Canon
John Blackburn*

This cameo is of the Rev. Canon John Blackburn. 1817-1852. During his time, the Parish Church was built and he became the first Vicar of Attercliffe. (You can see his wife's tomb at the top of the drive by the old church on Attercliffe Road.)

Before that date he held the Curacy at the Hill Top Chapel and cured the souls of all the people who lived in Attercliffe-cum-Darnall, Carbrook, parts of Grimesthorpe and Brightside.

Canon Blackburn had the Attercliffe Church School for girls and Infants built in 1824, two years before Christ Church opened. When the school was amalgamated with Lord Street National School (Leeds Road Church School) it housed the parochial office. In 1941 when the new church was bombed it became the new Attercliffe Parish Church. Canon Blackburn has such a commanding presence even in this photograph that I doubt anyone put anything past him during his time at the colliery, collecting evidence for the Commissioners (Children's Employment 1842.)

Houndsfield, Wilson & Co. held the lease on all the pits on The Common at the time Canon Blackburn was making his report. The Sunderland Moor Colliery took out the leases around 1865 with its 14 pits scattered over Attercliffe and Carbrook. The mining rights for all coal and minerals found under the ground belonged to the Duke of Norfolk or the Earls Wentworth and Fitzwilliam. William Staniforth and his mine at Darnall being the exception. The Tinsley Park pits were owned by Earl Fitzwilliam and were first sunk in 1811.

The mines were leased to the actual colliery owners through The Sheffield Coal Company and the small mines dotted around the area can be seen clearly on the Ordnance Survey Map of 1851, though all of the smaller ones were exhausted by then, leaving only the pits in Tinsley Park worked.

In the following report, Canon Blackburn gives a vivid account of the wretched lives of the children who worked at the colliery and at other trades. J.C.Symons Esq collected this and other accounts of children and working conditions in and around Yorkshire in the paper entitled **'Evidence on the employment of Children.'** (These papers may be viewed at the Local Studies Library, Surry Street.)

"There are about 60 colliers under 13 in this district. In one of the pits none but lads can hurry – the bed of coal being so shallow. The men are obliged to work on their side, or back or heel.

Little boys at six or seven of age blow the bellows for spade and shovel-makers. Six or eight boys of 8 or 9 years of age strike for the chain-makers; each man has a boy as a striker.

G.H. was a gin boy above ground at 5; a horse boy from the pit to the yard at seven; a ginnear under ground at the bull stake at 10; a loader and hurrier to the board-gate at 14.

Ginnears generally at 12 or 13; they stand at the bottom of the board-gate to take the full corves off the rope and to hang empty ones on. Fillers and hurriers push the corves down to the ginny or pully at the tip of the board-gate, formerly there were no railways: these have been introduced only within the last 30 years, before that time the boys had to hurry the corves with dog-belts. They push with their heads.

Fillers and Hurriers at 15 at High Hazels. Boys under 13 employed to take milk on donkies to Sheffield; their morals are very bad. Girls – only seldom employed to work in the pit, indeed so rarely that I know of only one family by which it has lately been practised – the father, mother, and girls all working below. This solitary instance has now vanished; they work above ground.

Girls under 13 are commonly employed to drive coal-carts, drawn by donkies or ponies, Girls in potteries and brickyards. Very young go from hence to Sheffield to work in hair seating manufactories. Girls not so young go into various manufactories in Sheffield – hardware, Britannia metal, silver-plating, button &c. &c. These are all sad demoralizing schools.

Potmakers under 13 work from 12 to 15 hours. Cutlers under 13 work from 13 to 14 hours. The collier lads work about 13 hours; from four or five a.m. to five or six p.m.

At some pits the boys generally go down at six. Some work all night, and play in the day. Some work shifts of 8 or 10 hours. No work is allowed on Sunday that can be avoided.

Before they go down, they breakfast on a 'bit of tea, or milk or porridge.' At night when they come out, the same – generally they have nothing but a piece of bread till they come out – seldom cheese. If a lad is fatherless the others always look at him, and make out for him. No boys look more at each other than colliers; if they see a boy without provision, they will say, "Hasn't got na dinner?" And they hand him a morsel of bread. Should any hang back they all cry out, 'Come, thou must gie him a bit and all.'

Many young persons of all ages, and all employments here die of consumption. Many go off in that way at 18 or 19.If a collier boy lives with his parents they receive the profit of the boy's labour till he is 21.A trapper (at 6 or 7 years old) has 3s. per week. A horse-boy 6s. or 7s. per week. Ginnear (11 or 12 yrs.old.) 7s. per week. Loader and hurrier (from18 yrs.) has from 5s. to 15s. per week. Colliers average from 7s. to 22s. (in former times 2 pound to 3 pound)"

The following statement was collected from a ten year old lad working at The Isle Pit in Tinsley Park in 1841, which was possibly the no. 2 pit marked on the 1903 O.S. map or the pits near the wharf at the end of Tinsley Park Road.

"I empty the corves and do the other light work to help my father. It's not hard work I do and I can stop whenever I'm tired. I've been to day school and a Sunday School. I could read in the New Testament when I left school; I can't write; I know I shall go to heaven if I'm good and to hell if I don't try to please God. Jesus was God's Son; He came to save sinners. I hear other boys swear some times and use bad language; but I never do myself."

The other main pit in the woods was The Peacock. In the 1840's the pit we knew as Tinsley Park was a Sandstone quarry and this was later utilized as a reservoir for the water pumped out of new shafts that were sunk on that site. When the mine finally closed c.1942 it was stocked with fish and became the Pump Pond familiar to many in the 1950's as a place for recreation.

Red Flags O'er The Common

It would be incomplete to end this brief look at Attercliffe in the 1840's without mentioning the political climate of the day. Encouraged by the unrest in Revolutionary France in the late 1790's, the disenfranchised of this country were beginning to air their grievances and unite around their political and trade union banners to protest against harsh anti-working class legislation and call for universal franchise. In the coalmines, wages and conditions were steadily deteriorating in the 1830's. Mine owners were ever ready to increase the size of the colliers' corves but not the rates of pay and the long hated method of paying wages out in over priced and shoddy goods at company shops, the Truck Payment system, was still in force.

The Combination Acts of 1799 and 1800 had prevented the meeting of two or more to bargain for wage increases and better conditions, though repealed in 1823 and 1824, (the latter only partially) still hung over them with its fear of Transportation.

Women and children had been banned from working underground by an Act of 1842 but many saw that as a way of preserving good wages for men only rather than any act of mercy aimed at removing women from places where they were in moral danger.

Social issues came to the fore as well. The feared Anatomy Act of 1832, which allowed the poor of the Work House to end up on the dissecting tables of the local hospitals, was a detested one and the chance to protest against this and the many injustices of the day came to the fore at the Great Rally in Sheffield in July 1844. They supported The Miners Strike of that year with such banners as: Britons Strike Home – Labour Is The Source Of All Wealth – Justice To All Privilege To None – Universal Suffrage – Wolves(Bishops)In Sheep's Clothing For They Devour Widow's Houses – Vote By Ballot-Thou Shall Never Vex The Stranger Nor Oppress Him – and Unite With Liberty And With Love. Sentiments universal in the Labour Movement down the centuries.

There was much civil unrest in our region in the 1830's. Indeed it could be said society was on the verge of civil war and the whole region was awash with foot soldiers and Dragoons (mounted soldiers with carbines) who charged around either intimidating the populace or attacking protesters. Attercliffe had strong links with the Chartist movement who saw universal franchise as the only way the working – man and woman could have a voice in the running of the country.

When he was first married, Sheffield's Chartist Leader Samuel Holberry had a home at Oakes Green Attercliffe with his wife's family, the Coopers. They then moved to Eyre Lane in Sheffield where he was arrested on the night of 11th January 1840 for planning armed insurrection. Holberry was sentenced to four years but died in prison two years into his sentence instantly becoming a martyr for the cause. The sight of cavalry charging up and down Attercliffe Common during these unsettled times must have been very frightening and very intimidating. Little wonder then the colliers of Hill Top and the other scattered mines in Carbrook and Top Common, had little stomach to fight the Sheffield Coal Company in the great strike of 1844 for very long, for they were small in number and a scattered community fearful for their jobs. A few at Tinsley Park did though and were summonsed for leaving their work and preventing others from attending theirs. Some protesters, notably one woman ran round the pit head Manager's Office holding aloft a red flag shouting –

'You've been Masters long enough – We'll be Masters Now!'

It is thought that because of the presence of the 'Attercliffe Friends' – political activists who at a minutes notice were ready to take part in armed struggle against the establishment of the day – and the geographical importance of Attercliffe as a half way point between Sheffield and Rotherham and thereby the rest of Britain – the magistrates saw fit to stable some of the extra forces that were brought in, (to supplement the contingent stationed at the Upperthorpe Barracks), at Hill Top on Attercliffe Common, to act as a deterrent to any would-be revolutionaries, and the authorities were well aware of the numbers they could muster for 40,000 people lined the streets as Holberry's cortege left his home at Oakes Green to The General Cemetery in Sheffield in 1842.

Though no evidence exists on paper to back this up, it has long been part of folk tradition and accepted by historians who have made a study of the Labour Movement in this district, and perhaps it was on Farmer Whitworth's land and stables on Hill Top Road that this took place -Who knows!!

Building the 'Cliffe

'The small tradesman, penurious in his habits, will not extend
a sixpence for the comfort of his tenants beyond necessity: and
the building clubs being composed of many, all having a
personal interest in the gains, but none of the comforts of their
tenants, will not allow of any expenditure beyond what
will secure tenants for the property.'

Workers Housing in West Yorkshire 1850-1920 Hobson

Speculative Builders, Landlords & Building Societies

Attercliffe was never a slum district like The Crofts or The Park districts of inner Sheffield. By the time the massive building programmes got under way in the 1860s, housing and the building of roads was standardised. Back-to-backs were banned in 1863. The new Bye-Law-Houses had two rooms downstairs with a front door and a back door to allow the passage of fresh air throughout the house to ensure the elimination of any trace of miasmas or foul air, that great bogey of Victorian planners who blamed this for the spread of such diseases as cholera.

Apart from the few back to back dwellings, the majority of the homes that went up in our district were Bye Law houses and were installed with water closets, though my no means all. Back to backs and other early housing had only pail closets that were emptied once or twice each week by the night-soil men who would remove each pail and tip the contents into the waiting cart parked by the kerbside. Folk who rented the yard houses of the back to backs had to put up with the sight and smell of the closets at their doors and windows, so their rents were lower. Rents for homes in Attercliffe at this time averaged between 1/6d and five shilling for a house, more if the house had a shop front. By the late 1960s, the house our family lived in on Coleridge Road was a two up and two down with an attic bedroom and the rent was 16/9d per week. Homes built from the 1850s onward remained untouched until Attercliffe was cleared in the 1970's.

In the 1862 edition of The Illustrated Guide to Sheffield, the publishers noted 'the thrift of at least a considerable part of the Sheffield artisan' in the district of Walkley, which enabled them through the prudent management of their finances to buy their own homes with the help of the Freehold Building Societies. Early building societies consisted of a group of men who pooled their savings, then they would draw a name out of a hat and that man would be the first to get his house built. This would go on until every man had a house. Then they became permanent building societies offering loans to buy land and the newly built homes to the wider public.

There have always been workers who are more frugal and thrifty than others. The majority of the Walkley artisans were from well-established families with well paid jobs and represented the upper working class. Compare them with the majority of Attercliffe and Carbrook folk who in a constant state of flux having just arrived from all over the British Isles to work in the steelworks, needed homes and needed them quickly. Providence which enabled the working man of Walkley to get a home by his own efforts also worked for the poor agricultural worker who came to the East End looking for work and homes, for they found both due to the prudence and management of speculative builders, investing landlords and the Building Societies.

Builders would have borrowed money to purchase land either freehold or leasehold and the money for the building materials. Then they would have sold them on to individual landlords who would have also borrowed money from the building society. The builders profits would have been immediate whereas the landlord would have waited some years before getting his loan paid back to the Society and then the profits from his rents would have been his alone. In The Illustrated Guide....., The Carbrook (First) Freehold Land Society is listed as expending the highest amount of money: £8,529.0.0, for the purchase of 189 lots. It is not easy to define the size of a lot without seeing the sales sheets. A lot could be one yard of four houses or two yards of six, but if by conjecture, all the lots were uniform that would put the cost of each lot at aprox. £45.2.6. If that were the case then these homes would have been very spartan indeed and perhaps included the back-to-backs on Carbrook Street that were the cheapest of all houses to build.

Building Societies have long been instrumental in the both the buying of land and in helping individuals to purchase them for occupancy or for renting out. A common practice

Particulars
Lot 1 A plot of land

Containing 10,860 square yards or thereabouts, situate in COLERIDGE ROAD (formerly Pot House Lane) Attercliffe, together with the MESSUAGE or DWELLING-HOUSE COW-HOUSE, SHED and OUTBUILDINGS thereon, occupied by Messrs Webster and Harvey. These buildings produce a gross annual rental of £33.12s.0d.

This lot is capable of being rapidly developed by the construction of Roads, as shown by the dotted line on the Plan hereto annexed. The making of the roads would open out the land and enable the whole of it to be utilized for building purposes, and the present time is a most favourable one, as *cottage houses are in great demand in Attercliffe.*

This land might also be utilized for tipping purposes before buildings are erected.

This lot will be sold subject to the right of way over the proposed road to be called Glave Street.

was for the purchaser to buy a row of houses and keep one of them for him or herself, usually the end one, and making it a more commodious building with possibly a bay window or more yard space than the others. He would then rent out the rest. Many landlords lived locally, some on the same street.

On the 1851 Ordnance Survey map, the only houses built on The Common with some sort of regime about them as opposed to the established dwellings of the pre-inclosure era, were a block of three cottages just beyond the Lambpool Inn and the newsagents next door. These were set back, having a small garden in front, and to the rear of these houses was a high wall separating them from Girton Road. Further down towards Carbrook was a run of shops and in the date stone set in the wall above Shaw's Mens & Boys Outfitters was the inscription *Carbrook Terrace 1854*. Does this mean Carbrook saw the first turf turned for the foundations of our homes? Certainly Lamb in *A Pub On Every Corner* dates the oldest purpose built public house in Carbrook as The Clifton on Clifton Street just off Broughton Lane built in 1774, with most of the other Carbrook pubs listed as being built in the 1860's, and where they be pubs, there be people!

Every possible use land had was never overlooked. Practises that are considered criminal today were acceptable in the 19th century. This sales sheet refers to land on Glave Street/Coleridge Road.

Miss— Broomhead Nightman & Moore

William Glave, deceased.

Particulars, Plan and Special Conditions of Sale

OF

VALUABLE FREEHOLD

BUILDING & TIPPING LAND,

DWELLING HOUSE AND COTTAGES,

SITUATE AT

ATTERCLIFFE, near SHEFFIELD,

TO BE

SOLD BY AUCTION,

BY

MESSRS. WILLIAM BUSH & SON,

AT THEIR AUCTION ROOMS, EAST PARADE, SHEFFIELD,

ON

Tuesday, 26th August, 1890,

At 4 o'clock for 4.30 in the Afternoon precisely.

F. PARKER RHODES,

Solicitor,

29, High Street, Rotherham.

Pawson and Brailsford, Printers, Sheffield.

Brown Bayley's later came to own the houses on the east side of The Common, and across the road the English Steel owned most. There were some, however, who paid their rent directly to their landlords at estate offices in Paradise Square and Norkolk Row. The estate agents for Attercliffe were Fernie, Greaves and Holland. All property repairs were reported to them via the rent man. Johnsons, Builders & Glaziers of Worksop Road then carried out the repairs. Their workmen pushed a hand-cart around the streets and according to one of their workmen they only did the absolute minimum in repairs. This same chap also states that some of the homes he worked in were so mucky there was grass growing under their sideboards!! One of my brothers who started his building career working for Longden's said he spent a lot of his time ripping out old fireplaces and some of the houses he worked in were so bad and the women so lazy they wouldn't even have the slop buckets out of the kitchen till dinner time!

The builders would replace loose slates, mend burst pipes and replace rotted guttering. Whenever gutters or other wood work was replace it never had a coat of paint or any kind of wood preservative, the wood just went up and stayed up until it in turn rotted and dropped off. I never saw anyone paint the outside of his or her house. Folk felt it was the property owner's responsibility, not theirs, but as they were too mean to spend a penny more than necessary it never got done.

I calculate my parents spent £1000 on their rents between the years 1933-1971, yet in all that time they only had about £5's worth of repairs done to their house.

Our landlords were just following tradition. As the social historian Hobson comments in *Workers Housing in West Yorkshire 1850-1920*.

> 'The small tradesman, penurious in his habits, will not extend a sixpence for the comfort of his tenants beyond necessity: and the building clubs being composed of many, all having a personal interest in the gains, but none of the comforts of their tenants, will not allow of any expenditure beyond what will secure tenants for the property.'

It wasn't unusual for women to have their names on the rent books though strictly speaking it should only have been the husband's name. I have come across generations of women living in the same house with their names only on the book. An old neighbour of ours on Coleridge always used to let her husband know when she'd had a few too many *'its my b******g name on the rent book not thine!'* Which was always the precursor to her husband's swift exit into the street! So women by tradition had equal rights to tenancy as men.

A sight familiar to us all – Johnson's work barrow on Berkley Road 1969.

(photo: Sheffield Newspapers)

There was however a disgraceful incident which took place on **Melville Road** in 1957 which was reported in the local press and the Church magazine. Two families who had recently been bereaved sent their rent books into the estate agents to have their homes transferred into the names of the deceased's son or daughter. These were families who had lived on the street for generations who had taken care of their homes and spent a lot of their own money modernizing them. The estate agents told them they would have to vacate their homes because the landlord had sold the houses, in one case to a young married couple. That wasn't the case; the new tenants were Asian men. No doubt the landlords got rent off each man thus making a very profitable transaction. I've always wondered how someone could come halfway around the world and land a tenancy. The Estate Agents were complicit in this unjust action and the incident I'm sure, did nothing for community relations.

In 1884 the leaseholds for all the houses on **Berkley Street** and surrounding streets came up for sale. The description on the Sales Sheet reads…

All or nearly all the Land was formerly waste or common, and the Property is sold subject to the provisions of the Attercliffe Enclosure Act and Award, and to the exceptions of Coal and Ironstone, and powers in relation thereto reserved on the Sale thereof to Mr Thomas Stead in 1867."

Thomas Steade was the main builder in Attercliffe and it is thought Steadfast Street is named after him. In Carbrook the Goulder Brothers were the main builders and their name is remembered in Goulder Place. The Amberley Hotel was built in 1860 and nearby on Cardiff Street were a few back-to-backs so I think it safe to assume that at least the land was purchased for building purposes and the laying out of the roads in the 1860's.

As for the houses themselves, perhaps an indicator may be found in the history of building work further along the Common and Attercliffe Road beginning at Newhall Road. The shops fronting Attercliffe Road between Newhall Road and Clay Street were begun in the late 1860's. The shops at the top of Leigh Street were built in the mid 1870's so progressing in the direction of Amberley Street, the houses on Berkley Street and Road were most likely to have been built in the late 1870's. The Ordnance Survey of 1881 shows both roads near complete.

All the houses on Berkley Street were well proportioned with bay windows and a small garden or space in front. Perhaps half the houses on the street had slop kitchens. As may be seen on the O.S. Map of 1905, most of the houses on this street had only two to a yard, which was very up-market for Attercliffe.

On the left hand side of **Berkley Road** as viewed from the main road was a run of four yards with four houses in each yard, then a break with a much shorter run with two yards. These were all three-bedroom houses with bay window. This first run had garret windows at the front. The gable ends between the two runs served as an entry.

On the right hand side there was a run of five yards with four houses in each then a break, then two yards, one with four houses and the top yard of three houses had access to **Blaco Road**. Only two of these houses had a slop kitchen and all had attic bedrooms except no 43, which for some reason didn't. The Levesley family who lived there in the 1950's thought the rent was around the 15/- per week mark.

One family on Berkley Road in the 1950's only had gas lighting in their house. Hanging from their ceiling was this curious contraption. It was a metal pipe with two upward curling mantle holders and a chain you pulled to light it and one to pull down to shut it off. This was all because the landlord of that particular run of houses was too mean to have electricity installed.

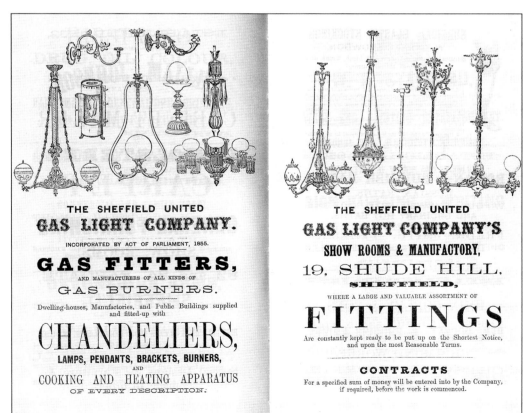

What a variety of styles and accommodation on these two roads, obviously the builder was providing homes to suit all pockets and all needs, and for the enterprising; shops with dwelling houses and extended business premises with stabling yards lining the main road.

The name Berkley was one of many names belonging to the Duke of Norfolk's family, as was Amberley. All the other names of roads in our area are place names or named after individuals. I have been unable to find the origins of Blaco.

Workmen's Cottages in Pothouse Lane 1871

Plan and Particulars

LEASEHOLD AND FREEHOLD PROPERTIES

AND

BUILDING LAND,

At ATTERCLIFFE, SHEFFIELD.

To be Sold by Auction,

BY

Messrs. NICHOLSON, GREAVES, BARBER, & HASTINGS,

AT THE

ESTATE SALE ROOM, HIGH STREET, SHEFFIELD,

ON

TUESDAY, JULY 15th, 1890,

At 4.30 p.m., subject to the Conditions of Sale to be then produced:—

LEASEHOLD.

LOT 1. SEVENTEEN DWELLING-HOUSES,

Numbered 61 to 75, in Coleridge road; 58 to 72, in Edward road; and 3 and 5, in Pothouse road, producing a gross Annual Rental of £169. 1s. 0d.

The Site contains 907 square yards, or thereabouts, and is held under Lease for 800 years, from 1872, at the Annual Ground Rent of £26. 2s. 8d.

LOT 2. TWELVE DWELLING-HOUSES,

Numbered 49 to 59, in Coleridge road, and 46 to 56, in Edward road, producing a gross Annual Rental of £117. 0s. 0d.

The Site contains 779 square yards, or thereabouts, and is held under Lease for 800 years, from 1872, at the Annual Ground Rent of £18. 8s. 4d.

LOT 3. TWELVE DWELLING-HOUSES,

Numbered 37 to 47, in Coleridge road, and 34 to 44, in Edward road, and the WORKSHOP in the Yard, the whole producing a gross Annual Rental of £118. 19s. 0d.

The Site contains 782 square yards, or thereabouts, and is held under Lease for 800 years, from 1871, at the Annual Ground Rent of £18. 12s. 4d.

LOT 4. TWELVE DWELLING-HOUSES,

Numbered 25 to 35, in Coleridge road, and 22 to 32, in Edward road, and the WORKSHOP in the Yard, the whole producing a gross Annual Rental of £118. 19s. 0d.

The Site contains 765 square yards, or thereabouts, and is held under Lease for 800 years, from 1871, at the Annual Ground Rent of £18. 2s. 8d.

LOT 5. TWELVE DWELLING-HOUSES,

Numbered 13 to 23, in Coleridge road, and 10 to 20, in Edward road, producing a gross Annual Rental of £117.

The Site contains 775 Square Yards or thereabouts, and is held under Lease for 800 years from 1871, at the Annual Ground Rent of £18. 7s. 4d.

Lots 1 to 5 form one Block of Property, and being near to the Works of Messrs. Brown, Bayley (Limited), and Messrs. S. H. Burrows and Co., and to Attercliffe Common, are always let.

The houses under study in this section is really the study of Attercliffe in microcosm, and an insight into the planning, building and maintenance of what were described as 'Workmen's Cottages' which were 'always let' as they were so near the tenants place of work.

These houses formed a block between Edward Road and Coleridge Road. They were something hard to visualize today being three roomed houses with one room on top of the other and a cellar below ground level. The plan on the opposite page gives the impression of an extension on the back but this represented a small kitchen tacked on to the parlour on the ground floor with a corrugated steel roof. On the first floor was the parent's bedroom with the children's bedroom in the garret above that.

A garret was a bedroom built in the roof space but with a half sized window on the front of the house, whereby an attic was a bedroom in the roof space but with a skylight on the roof. Both types of bedroom were remarkably spacious with room to sleep three to four persons.

It is hard to imagine, but some couples shared these homes with other couples and extended families often shared the meagre accommodation with relatives. Though common it was strictly speaking illegal and printed on the front of every rent book were the words -No sub-letting allowed. Making good use of the land available was something Victorian builders were very good at. It also made good economic sense at the time.

'When there was room to build a terrace only one house deep,
this sometimes resulted in the half-back or 'salt pie' house,
built as a back to back but without the rear dwelling and
therefore with only a single pitch roof.'

(Workers housing in West Yorkshire.1850-1920.)

These house were double pitched though, certainly the photographs I have seen of them suggest they were. Their back yards were very spacious but the ones I saw weren't paved or tarmac'd, just compounded black grit. Half way up the backs of these houses were small windows that gave a bit of daylight to the top of the staircase but looked as if they were put in as an afterthought. I always referred to them as blind- back houses thinking this was as appropriate a name as any, for as they were originally built without any lights on the back then they would have looked blind.

They seemed to be just the front part of back-to-backs with a small slop kitchen tacked on to the back, I think more for stability than anything else.

These homes were a bit of a puzzle though; half-backs were an economical solution where land was at a premium, but on this site there was room to build the bigger Bye-Law homes. Most likely the builder wanted to build homes as cheaply as possible for country folk used to living in one- room cottages that were at the cheaper end of the rented market. Back-to-backs were a cheaper form of housing and a few were built on nearby Swan Street. Sheffield Council had placed a ban on them in 1863 so this option wasn't available to our builder on this site.

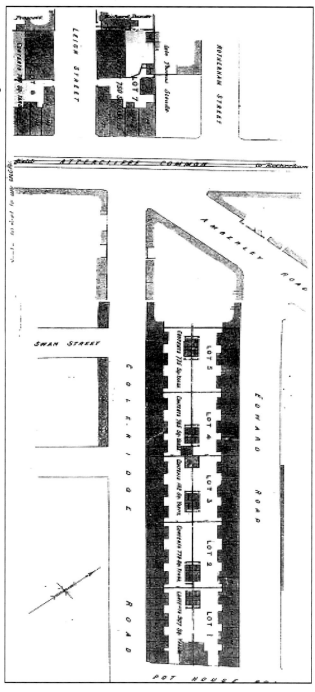

The houses were built with very poor bricks called *chuffs*. Seconds, as builders joked were used only because they couldn't get their hands on thirds! The best building bricks come from Stairfoot near Barnsley, which are considered better than London bricks. I'd like to think these bricks were produced locally maybe in the Old Pottery or if not then at any one of the brick-yards dotted around the area. Street furniture such as lamp-posts were cast at the Eagle Foundry near Stevenson Road. Just imagine between the eighteen fifties and early nineteen hundreds Attercliffe must have been one huge building site.

The whole street that faced us on Coleridge was in such a precarious state that iron rods were pushed through some of the houses at intervals. These rods had a plate at the back and front and were bolted on. I suppose this was to stop the walls from splaying out. These rods ran through the living room. Nowadays, if a building is thought to be unsafe then the tenants would be moved out instantly and put in emergency accommodation. How did our neighbours of yesteryear cope with such a calamity? Why, they just hung their washing on them to dry! Was that true Yorkshire Grit or not?

All these homes were demolished in 1962.

Rents for the Half-Back houses on Coleridge, Amberley, Edward and Pothouse Roads in 1890.

Lots 3,4, and 5 were the first to go up in 1871. Lots 1 and 2 went up in 1872.

Taking **Lot 1** as a sample to work out the rents, the seventeen houses in the two yards produced a gross annual rent of £167/1/0d.That works out at 3/9d per week for the houses on the left and right hand side of the yards. The two houses facing Pothouse Road being slightly bigger perhaps fetched a weekly rent of 4/0d per week.

Lot 5 has twelve dwelling houses in two yards fronting Coleridge Road and Edward Road. These bring an annual gross rental of £117/-/-. This works out at 3/9d per week. The folk in **Lot 2** paid 3/9d per week in rent.

The two homes in **Lot 3** that rented a workshop as well as his house paid 7/6 a week on top of the rent making it 11/3d per week! This seems exceptionally high as there is no access for horse and cart to enable the tenant to run a business. Also note the type of privy in these yards. These were either a 'pail closet' that had a bucket under the seat that was emptied by the night soil men once or twice a week, or the 'midden' type where the refuse was removed by shovel and carried away in a tub to the waiting cart by the road.

(Regarding this chapter – I wouldn't say my arithmetic was brilliant so if there's someone out there who has worked out a different figure for these rents it would be good to hear from you. A.S.)

Carbrook – The Formative Years

The back yard industries of scissor making, pocket knife making, file cutting, farming and mining which marked the years up to 1860 now gave way to the great steel works with their attendant housing that swallowed up the remaining portions of our district. Attercliffe had grown at a remarkable rate. The Census Returns for 1841 showed a population of 4,156. By 1881 it had soared to 26,965. The homes built during this period were in the main purchased by local businessmen or publicans as small investments with no means or intention of maintaining them or making periodical improvements. The Public Health Act of 1864 called for work on sewer construction, but this was not completed until 1886 when Blackburn Meadows sewage works opened. Before this the emptying of privy middens had to be paid for and the night soil taken to the tip at the top of Terry Street on land that eventually became the Recreation Ground.

Between 1871 and 1881, 3,010 homes had been built in Carbrook. The author Parsons comments that these homes were "built initially on the back to back principle arranged around courts." (c.f. Schools in an Urban Community p.3). This is in my opinion too much of a generalisation as back to backs represented only a very small percentage of the various house and shop types in Carbrook built concurrently from the early 1850's onwards. To my personal knowledge, there were none built around courts in our district as they were say in The Park district.

The poverty experienced by country folk in the 'hungry forties' drove the farm labourers to the industrial north to seek a better life. Communal poverty did though produce a kinship of sorts out of the diverse mixture of migrants that came from all the corners of the kingdom to settle the new district and was one that continued for generations with the poor always giving a helping hand to those even poorer on their doorstep. Where government charity was either not forthcoming or rejected, locals cared for each other with door to door collections for funerals or with the local Working Men's Clubs giving children a day out in the country. The practice of grandparents bringing up their children's children in separate households was so common as to be the norm.

The itinerant or temporary workers were also catered for in the hostels erected during the latter part of the nineteenth century. The big building at the top of Weedon Street was one, and during the thirties was known as 'The Doss House', as was the Union at Carbrook in its final years. The Carlton Hotel near Washford Bridge and The Hallamshire Coffee House on The Common by Coleridge Road served those with a bob or two and for the travelling salesman there was the Amberley Hotel, the biggest hotel on The Common. By far the greatest provider of homes though was the ordinary family who made room for 'the lodger'.

The need to school the children of the newly arrived workers led to the opening of Carbrook C. of E. (National) School in January 1870. Memories from the school's first years come from Mr Cornthwaite, who was Headmaster, writing in 1957:

> "In one of the school records, the headmaster has written a note
> describing how as he sat in the school he could hear the lively rattle
> of harvesting machines in the fields around the school. Who has also
> seen the ponds in those fields covered with a thick layer of ice
> (for winters seemed harder in great grandmamma's days) on which
> the boys used to extend quite unlawfully their dinner hour, much to the
> annoyance of the master, whose wrath and rod served to provide a
> sudden warmth in certain places as a reminder of their need to
> return to school promptly."

A temporary school in the Clifton Street United Methodist chapel opened in 1872 and taught both juniors and infants until the new Carbrook Board School opened in 1874. Although the school rolls were full after a few weeks of each school opening it had always been difficult keeping the children attending on a regular basis. Harvesting and potato picking were the main work based excuse of absentees with Saint Monday and local feast days being the others. As The National School was not supported by the Rates they had to charge each pupil a penny or two each week. Because of this it had trouble keeping hold of its pupils from the 1880's onwards, as these decades were marked by depression, want and industrial unrest.

With a population still on the increase and experiencing severe poverty the Education Board was compelled to build yet more schools. The second Carbrook Board School opened in 1889 – the junior school of our day and Tinsley Park Road School – Coleridge Road Boys' School of our day opened in 1896.

Home Comforts, Cleanliness & Moderate Charges

THE

Hallamshire Coffee House Co.

LIMITED,

HEELEY, ROTHERHAM, ECKINGTON, CARBROOK.

Attention is directed to the houses of the Company, which are open for the use of the public, and specially suited for the accommodation of Cyclists, Commercial Travellers, &c.   [C.T.C. appointments.]

"HALLAMSHIRE" TEMPERANCE COMMERCIAL HOTEL.

OPPOSITE GENERAL POST OFFICE, ROTHERHAM.

BED, BOOTS and ATTENDANCE   -   -   1/6 and 1/9

BILLIARDS.   AIRY ROOMS.

"HALLAMSHIRE" COFFEE HOUSES

AT

20, WESTGATE, ROTHERHAM;

SOUTHGATE, ECKINGTON;

HEELEY BRIDGE, NEAR MIDLAND STATION, HEELEY;

AND

ATTERCLIFFE COMMON (CORNER OF COLERIDGE ROAD), ATTERCLIFFE.

Billiards, Games, Beds, Breakfasts, Dinners, Luncheons, Teas, Lavatories, Ladies' Rooms, &c., at all the houses.

SECRETARY TO THE COMPANY,

H. WELLS-SMITH, C.A., 8, Bank Street, SHEFFIELD.

In the brickwork above Shaw's of Carbrook was a stone inscribed with the words – *Carbrook Terrace 1854*. In the 1950's Shaw's was the leading Gents and Boy's outfitters. When you went there to buy a shirt the assistant would pull open a drawer and lift two or three out for the customer to choose from. Then the item would be wrapped in brown paper and string. Another shop of note to open in Carbrook was the very first Co-Op in Sheffield; The Brightside & Carbrook on Bright Street opened in 1868 on the corner of Bright Street and Carbrook Street. A more grandiose building was erected across the road some years later and became The Brightside & Carbrook Central Stores & Offices.

Wesleyan Methodist Church Carbrook Street built in 1870. Looking to the junction with Dunlop Street and the Industry on its corner. The run of properties in this shot are back-to-backs with nine homes facing the road and nine up the entry. Contrary to popular belief there weren't that many back-to-backs in Carbrook. The upper rooms in this church would have been used by the Sunday School and may have been built on the same design as the **Princess Street Wesleyan Methodist Church and Day School** built in 1868 serving that little crowded community with places for 700 children.

Carbrook Conservative Club – Bowling Green on Bright Street 1897

The occasion is Queen Victoria's Jubilee in 1897. Behind the tent is the Bethel Sunday School Bright Street built 1861 which was directly behind the Chapel facing Attercliffe Common. The row of houses on the left are on Bright Street and the gable end in the middle is Dunlop Place. The houses here seem to be very well built, attractive properties. They were pulled down when The English Steel expanded its works. In the second frame the children in their Sunday best go for tea in the marquee.

Clifton Street Methodist Church with Carbrook Church in the background

The Bethel Primitive Methodist Chapel – Attercliffe Common built 1867

Opposite Goulder Place. This photograph was taken before the front was enlarged in the late 1920's to become The Wesley Central Hall. Their Sunday School fronted Bright Street and was built some years earlier in 1861. When the church closed in 1957 it became a Roller Skating Rink. The Methodist built many attractive chapels in our district. Theirs was a very simple and graceful style of architecture. The main feature in chapels is the pulpit and there by The Word, with Anglicans it is The Altar with its emphasis on the Holy Communion. Non-Conformist named their Chapels after places in the Old Testament. The minister here was the Rev. Surtees.

SALEM – A variation of Jerusalem, The Holy City.

BETHEL – Hebrew for 'house of God'. An ancient town near Jerusalem. A home for Christians.

ZION – The hill on which Jerusalem stands, a religious society or its site, an ideal Christian community.

BETHESDA – The pool of healing in Jerusalem.

EBENEZER – Hebrew for 'a stone of help' A memorial stone blessed by Samuel in memory of a great victory over the Philistines.

SHILOH – A town in Canaan where the Ark and tabernacle were kept. Destroyed by the Philistines.

TABERNACLE – A portable tent or shrine where the divine presence dwelt. A sanctuary where the Ark of the Covenant was kept. A meeting place for Non-Conformists.

Although from a chapel further up Attercliffe this advertisement would have attracted a large congregation, especially as Sankey's hymns were on the programme. The Scots evangelist was famous for his hymns and his collaboration with the American evangelist Moody. In their day they were the Lennon & McCartney of the Church World.

The Last Back to Backs in Attercliffe

There were not many back-to-back houses in Attercliffe and the only one I ever went inside was on Carbrook Street. The year would have been 1955. It was the home of school friend Rene Daly and I thought how exciting it must have been to open a cupboard door and climb a narrow flight of stairs to bed. But it was not so romantic to discover that in order to go to the lavatory you had to exit the front door on to Carbrook Street, turn left up an entry then walk across a yard. The last time I stepped into this type of dwelling was in 1998 when I discovered these on Washford Bridge. Were they the last back-to-backs to be demolished in Atttercliffe?

They were part of a run between Stoke Street and Washford Bridge and were built c.1860. They were demolished in Dec.1999. The shop was a beer-off and the jennell at the left side led to a courtyard and The Grey Horse on Stoke Street behind.

Some of the original fixtures were still intact, on the front the wood surrounds at the door and shop window look like the originals. At the back the window frames on the ground floor are original as is the door with the plywood cover half removed. Actually looking at the brickwork at the back I would say, although 150 years old, looked in better condition than a house we lived in that was only up for 55 yrs. The condition of a house depends only on the way it is looked after by the landlord.

The rooms in the back-to-back properties were very small by today's standards, barely 10ft x 10ft; they may have been smaller. They had the modern type of Yorkshire Range, the ones that were cream coloured as opposed to the older black ones so someone may have modernised this house at some point.

There was a butler sink in the alcove beside the chimney-breast. Above the sink was a cupboard with glass doors. It was the same as the one we had in our first house that was built around 1900. There were two doors inside the room, one led to the cellar and the other, that looked like a cupboard door, was actually the door that opened on to a flight of stairs to the first floor bedroom.

In A History of Old Attercliffe, Vine records a builder from the Park district who built the homes on Washford Bridge in the early 1860s. The rents for houses facing the streets were 2/6d a week and the homes behind facing the yard and privies 1/6

per week. Other rents in this district were 2/9d a week and for some between 2/7d and 5/4d per week. For some 'tenements' on Faraday Rd the rents were between 1/6d and 2/6d. (c.f. Vines History of Attercliffe p.90-93.)

This type of house was unfairly maligned in my opinion. They offered the migrant from the countryside immediate and affordable housing in a style they were familiar with i.e. the one room cottage.

This view shows the backs of the houses. The wall has the remains of an advertisement for John Smith's Tadcaster Ales. This house was built in a peculiar wedge shape which was due to it being built on an ancient boundary line that ran at an angle to the road.

 An interesting aside here, a lady who grew up across the road from here on Harriet Road, Mrs Clarke, said the first coloured family she ever knew, the Peters family lived in this yard and that would have been in the 1920's. This is interesting because a newspaper report of 1896 tells the case of a juvenile who was fined for breaking lamp- lights with a catapult. He was a coloured youth from off Carlisle Street and his family name was Peters. Coupled with the fact that I knew of a coloured family in Carbrook named Peters also in the 1950's. Could they all have been members of the same extended family?

EMMANUEL CHURCH,

SHEFFIELD.

Hymns for Whitsuntide,

1893.

SHEFFIELD:

PAWSON AND BRAILSFORD, PRINTERS, &c., HIGH-ST. AND MULBERRY-ST,

1893.

Hymn Sheet for Emmanuel Church Washford Bridge dated Whitsuntide 1893. This is the only picture I have every seen of Emmanuel church which was built in 1882. The church was bombed during The Blitz and only the Church Hall was left standing. Out of the four Parish Churches in Attercliffe, three were bombed, which seemed more than a little unfair. The congregation was transferred to Christ Church Attercliffe, and its famous Youth Club decamped to the Leeds Road National School site in the mid 1950's. In the engraving can be seen a horse drawn tram heading towards Washford Bridge and looking slightly out of proportion. The original tram-line from Lady's Bridge to The Golden Ball was laid in1873 and was extended to Carbrook in 1874. Before that date a private company ran a horse omnibus service from Hillsborough to Attercliffe in 1852. The fare was 3d. (This leaflet came from FAV Carr – Head Mistress of Carbrook County Infant's School. It was her family's place of worship when they lived on Makin Road).

A Little History of The Rec

Philip & Martin Arundel with little girl from Terry Street 1973

Don't you know it seems a shame,

You don't know what you've got 'till its gone;

Pave Paradise and put up a parking Lot.

(with apologies to J. Mitchell)

PRESENTED BY.
MR. ARTHUR WIGHTMAN.

1st March 1887 (R)

PARTICULARS

OF

FREEHOLD BUILDING LAND

AND

Dwelling = Houses

Known as "BELLE VUE," situate at

ATTERCLIFFE COMMON, SHEFFIELD,

TO BE

SOLD BY AUCTION,

BY

Messrs. WM. BUSH & SON,

At their Mart, East Parade, Sheffield,

On TUESDAY, the 1st of MARCH, 1887,

AT FOUR O'CLOCK IN THE AFTERNOON,

Subject to Conditions of Sale.

PARTICULARS.

Lot 1.

A PLOT OF LAND,

Containing about 1a. 1r. 26p., bounded north by Attercliffe Board Schools, east by Lot 2, south by land of Mr. Steade, and west by Tinsley Road (Attercliffe Common).

Lot 2.

A PLOT OF LAND,

Containing about 4a. 3r. 2p., bounded north in part by lands of Mr. J. F. Swallow and the M. S. & L. Ry. Co. respectively, east by land of the M. S. & L. Ry. Co., south by land of Mr. Steade, and west in part by Lot 1 and in part by the Board Schools; together with the RANGE OF HOUSES called "Belle Vue,"—the main house being occupied by Mr. Geo. Green, and the cottages by Messrs. Pawson, Nutt, Mincher and Parkin. This plot is particularly eligible for a **JUBILEE RECREATION GROUND.**

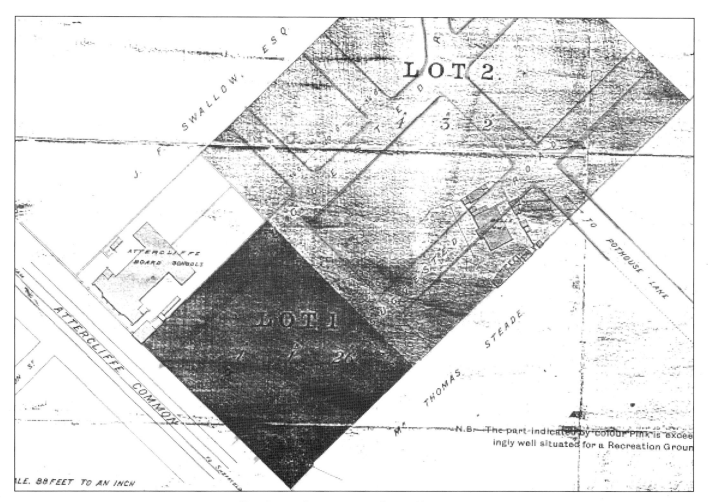

Carbrook Recreation Ground

LOT 2

This area of land that was to become Carbrook Recreation Ground was first suggested as a Jubilee Recreation Ground around 1887 at the time of Queen Victoria's Jubilee, and had previously been used as dumping ground for "night soil" – that lovely euphemism for the stuff that came flying off a shovel fast in the middle of the night and was carted away whilst everyone was abed. Perhaps this is why The Rec. always produced a good crop of flowers. There used to be an old coal mine at the top of Carltonville Road and one at the back of The Rec., by the Co-Op Garages. I wonder what the infill might have been?

The house plan that can just been seen on the sales map was Belle View and once the home of a famous engineer Joseph Locke, who built the Woodhead Tunnel. Another occupant was Steven Terry, a local publican, who gave his name to the street leading up to his house. The original plans for the area covered by the Carbrook Rec. were to be by the looks of it, for more houses and streets. Goodness, people must have been arriving in Attercliffe by the trainload.

Now the cynics amongst you may wonder why valuable building land was proposed as a recreation ground? Well the Victorians did produce their fair share of philanthropist. Thomas Firth the steelworks magnate purchased a sizable portion of land at Firth Park and presented it to the people. At Carbrook, according to the sign by the Rec. gates he was also the main contributor in the purchase of this land for use as a much needed place of recreation.

LOT 1 was purchased by the Sheffield School Board for the building of Carbrook County Junior School in 1889, and the laying out of Terry Street.

Carbrook Recreation Ground c. 1900

Attercliffe is to have something tangible, if not in the shape of a public park,
in the form of a greatly needed Recreation ground, which is something
more than a pestilential bed of disease. Our recreation grounds are mostly
supplied with gymnasiums, swings etc., but we understand the
Recreation and Parks Committee have resolved to decorate
Carbrook Grounds with trees and shrubs at the cost of £1,000
in addition to gymnasiums, provision will be made for cricket and football.'

(Whitaker's Attercliffe Almanack. 1880.)

The earliest photo I have ever seen of Carbrook Rec. Here we see Sunday-School scholars from the local Chapels, their banners fluttering in the breeze. The Junior Department of Carbrook School is on the right with the open space of the schoolyard separating it from Terry Street. Thurley Place and Scoften Place can be seen on the extreme left. This photo is, going by the fashions from 1900-1910, and the fact that the junior department was opened in 1889.

This is where the traditions of Christian Witness at Whitsuntide and the older pagan Rites of Spring reflected in the crowning of The May Queen, were carried from the countryside to the industrial heartlands of the north.

When Attercliffe disappeared in the 1970's they were not allowed to take this tradition to the new housing estates with them. These new estates were sterile in every sense of the word. In order to get to a church, chapel, pub or social club for that matter, you would have to have a car. Where we lived, we could have reached any one of these places within minutes from our front door on foot. The old ways were firmly nailed in the coffin by town planners with hostile political attitudes towards churchgoers. The Sunday Schools and Youth Clubs we attended were all in a sorry state in the 1950's and 60's and received no outside help in renovating the old premises or indeed rebuilding. On the other hand leafltets were displayed in Attercliffe Library in the 60's asking anyone who wanted to turn their front room into a 'prayer room' should contact the council for help.

Kids in The Rec. 1950-1975

Left to right: Jean Gregg, Mavis Sapcote, Audrey Outram, Molly Gregg, Ann Leversidge.

I'd like to thank all those who kept The Rec. open and the Parks Department for all the wonderful floral displays and for entertaining us each summer with Punch & Judy Shows. For the playground, the football and cricket-pitch, the bowling green and the tennis courts.

We also had the Whit Parades and concerts where local kids would sing or recite poems or dance. We were never out of there; it must have been a godsend to our mothers. I can honestly say that I spent more time in The Rec than I did at home. Funnily enough, the last social group to occupy this land were the travellers. When they camped there in the late 80's no one could get on the old Rec because of their dogs; massive Irish Wolf Hounds and Greyhounds, all of them scabby with lumps missing off their heads. They too used The Rec as a repository for night soil! Locals who lived and worked on Broughton Lane at the time got so fed up of ringing the police to complain about them making their calls of nature 'au natural' as it were. They gave up. Was this a case of history repeating itself?

In the height of summer, the park keeper would turn his hosepipe on us and within minutes there would be scores of kids in swimming gear running around wet through and loving every minute of it. This was where our holidays were spent, not at Blackpool or Scarborough. Our Mum took us to other parks too during the long summer holidays – Millhouses, Endcliffe and Clifton Park in Rotherham.

Not long after the war the government decided to build more nursery schools so that mothers could go back to work. The one in The Rec was built in 1951. This photo was taken on the spot where this new nursery was built. Its entrance was at the top of Manningham Road but could also be accessed through The Rec itself. I went there in 1951 before going to Carbrook County Infants.

From left to right are:- ?, Audrey Outram, Brian Sapcote, Ann Sapcote,?, Rita Standish.
In the background is Carltonville Road.

Whitsuntide in The Rec. 1954

Terry Street at the Junction with Attercliffe Common. The lorries carrying the May Queen and her Attendants are leaving The Rec and going back to the Chapels on Whit Monday. Local lorry firms like Robert Earl of Amberley Road, used to loan their flat backed wagons free of charge for the occasion. All of the houses on Terry Street and those pictured here on the corner with the Common were well built and well kept. The ones on Terry St. even had a bit of a garden and front gate, also a slop kitchen on the back. Can you see the Ovaltine Lady on the advertisement board?

By the gates at Blaco Road. In the background – Thurley Place and Scoften Place.
The girls are: Ann Hillery, Ann Sapcote, Cynthia Hillery with Mrs Hillery holding our coats.

May Queen and Attendants.

The pageant is carried on in the yards of Brompton Road. These children went to Clay Street Methodist Chapel. They are left to right:- Janis Brooks, Sylvia Cutts, Josephine Standcliffe and ? Dalton.

This is what Whitsuntide meant to us in the 1950's. The only time we had new clothes we would parade in The Rec and visit relations and have a few pennies put in our new handbags.

Pictured here are Janis Brooks (Brompton Road) and Pat Turner whose parents had the Newsagent's shop at the top of Newhall Road.

Paradise Lost

It was on this day in 1973 I saw Miss Renshaw for the last time. Keeping a long tradition she was organizing the Annual Sports Day for the few remaining children going to Carbrook Infants School. The junior dept. of our old school had been closed in 1971and the children transferred to Huntsman's Gardens and now renamed The Carlton School.

This was rather a pathetic sight with perhaps a dozen children taking part, they can actually been seen in the background as can Miss R. just over my right shoulder. As always Beryl was wearing an outfit with matching nail varnish and lipstick in her favourite colour – siren red.

The Brownhill Sisters in The Rec, Whitsuntide c.1951 record their memories.

We lived at no 47 Belmoor Road. We also had some cousins who lived on Blaco Road. Their names were Barbara, Irene, Jimmy and Peter Moffatt, also our Auntie Shirley Robertson. We were all brought up in the area of Carbrook Recreation Ground and we used to have some good times in there in the school holidays, and our parents knew we would be safe because the park keeper Mr Barratt used to keep his eye on us and all the kids that played there. The people we remember that lived round about us were Mavis Webster, Iris Young, Ivy Howe, Jacqueline Heppinstall and Margaret Hill. We wonder where they all are now. We live at Handsworth and come to the new ice skating rink regularly to have a cup of coffee and look out of the big windows on the back overlooking what was Blaco Road. (Sandra married one the Oliver Bros. who ran the chain of butchers shops on the Cliff.)

Note: Mr Andrew Barrett was the most well known and loved park keepers in the Rec. When he died on August 16th 1952, neighbours crowded round the gates at Terry Street and Blaco Road on the day of his funeral to pay their respects and watch him leave his home at the lodge for the very last time.

The Old Man's Hut at the top of the Rec. Next to it was the shelter but it was a brave soul who kicked a ball around in there or made a noise generally. You would have been beaten to death with walking sticks. The old men who sat in there to play cards or keep warm by the old stove would put up with no nonsense from any kids!

The buildings behind it were part of the Co-Op Dairy that faced Broughton Lane. Pictured here is Martin Arundel in 1973.

The Long Goodbye

The flower-beds long removed. Compare this with another picture of neglect that is The Rec a few years later. Looking at these haunting pictures, it's not hard to imagine our district's rural past with sheep grazing on the Common. Given any chance Mother Nature always takes back her own. The Rec had a gymnasium when it first opened. It was on the site of the nursery opened in 1951. Every day the children were lined up in the hall and fed cod-liver oil and malt off the spoon. I swear it was the same spoon for everyone!

Above: The Rec in 1988 looking a bit like Top Witherns. Listen! Can you hear someone calling……..………'Heath---cliffe'.

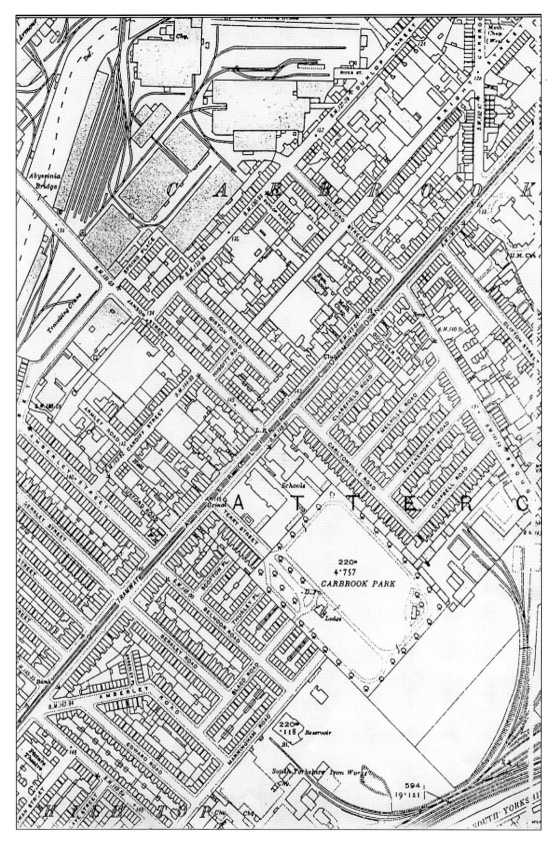

The Rec complete as we knew it. In the heart of Carbrook and a place we all keep in our hearts. As kids, we played in it right round the clock. When we were courting we walked out with our boy/girl friends arm in arm, as mothers we pushed our prams around it when baby needed some fresh air and when they were older they took themselves there and so the whole thing turned full cycle. You'd think because of all the wrongs done to us by town planners they could at least give back The Rec as is was in the 1950's, a park with all its amenities with perhaps a bas-relief in bronze by the gates at Terry Street depicting the countless generations of working families who took time from their labours to enjoy this little demi-paradise on their doorstep.

Once Round the Lump

*It is also a history of that part of Attercliffe where we lived,
the bustling chaotic and hilarious lives of its inhabitants
and more important, of our place in its history, of where we
lived, played and went to school and of the homes we grew up
in and street we played in, where after being called in at dusk
we were always allowed one more run around the lump
before going to bed.*

Our Lump

Any block of houses where you lived was your lump. Small when you were an infant, it grew, as you got older. As very small children, our lump was up Manningham, left down Belmoor, left again down Blaco then left again on to Amberley and back at our starting point. The lump was where we ran our races, skipped, trolley-ed or walked round on stilts and sometimes, on hot summer days, paid a penny to be driven round in Malcolm Stuart's pony and trap.

Our bit of Carbrook was built with some thought to the street layouts. No street was longer than 100 yards without an interesting corner or place to turn into. Looking at a map, it seems that even in Victorian times the modern concept of Feng-Shui played its part in the shaping of our streets. Not here the never ending roads of Parson Cross or the everlasting circles of The Manor.

Coleridge Road, Attercliffe Common, Carbrook Recreation Ground and Brown Bayley's Steel Works that separated us from the incline at the Pothouse Bridge and the cut of the canal beyond bounded this area where I lived until 1956. There was always a foul smell from Brown Bayley's pickling tanks on the opposite side of the road and an ear shattering noise when the steam pressure on the big hammer in the East Forge was released. While this was going on no one could hear a thing that was being said and we used to put our fingers in our ears until it had stopped. This steam pressure was the driving force of a 5 ton hammer that was worked 24 hours a day.

The Sheffield Butchers' Hide & Skin Co originally owned the house I was born into at 17 Manningham Road in 1947. My mother remembers paying rent to them when she was first married in 1933. Her next-door neighbour, Mrs Baxter, who was older than mother, remembered the road before it was fully built up saying that it was always strewn with broken pottery. Now, whether or not these were remnants from the Old Pottery or left over from the builders, we don't know.

I am one of seven children and I suppose it's thanks to the incompetence of the Luftwaffe navigators that my family and I are alive today, for if any bombs had hit the steelworks then all our houses would have gone up with them.

At the beginning of the war, mum had two children and was expecting her third when she was given notice to evacuate to a village in Lincolnshire; but she wouldn't go. I don't think Dad could have coped one day without her. Their cellar was cleaned out by some council workmen, who said that all the cellars in their yard were extremely dry due to them being built on clay. This was used as an air-raid shelter. People living further up the road though had Anderson shelters built in their back yards. My childhood then was spent in this two up two down terrace house opposite Brown Bayley's Forge and the noise, the constant thud from the big hammer was my companion ever since I could remember, though it wasn't as you'd imagine a frightening noise, more a soothing reassurance that all was well; it was after all my first noise, a muffled heartbeat a baby hears when its being nursed. The noise seemed to transmit through the ground and the brickwork so it was felt as well as heard and every night the window frames gently rattled to its thump, thump. When we moved to Coleridge Road in 1956 we were to miss this, not as if there wasn't enough noise to compensate for this particular one but the standing joke in our family was that no one could get to sleep because it was so quite.

The first light of day used to struggle to make its presence felt, competing with the soot grime and ashes that flew around the house when mother was trying to resurrect the previous nights fire coaxing and begging it to burn with pages from The News of The World. Mum recalled an instance when Dr Wainwright walked straight in at the front door, no knock or anything, saying what an earth did she think she was doing black-leading the stove when she was only 'two days'. Mother was in fact buffing up the range with scrunched up sheets of newspaper and she explained it wasn't her that had just had a baby but the woman next door.

Our kitchen floor was covered with great slabs of red and black tiles. They were usually covered with rugs except on washday when they were taken out and hung over the back wall. By the side of the small range was a set-pot. A set-pot was an extension of the chimney-breast, a place to heat water with a space under where you made a fire. It had a wooden lid that you would remove to fill with water and put in clothes that needed a boil. After each washday mother would save the soapy water in the set-pot and stand me first then my brother in to bath us. Mother had a small Hoover single tub, but she still used a mangle, dolly tub, ponsher, washboard and bluebags. For soap she would scrape bits off a long block of green soap, this would dissolve in the hot water and bubble up really well. At bath time we had red carbolic soap. Thin wedges were cut off long blocks and we were scrubbed with loofahs. We used to come out of the bath looking like boiled lobsters. For the baby though, we were sent out to buy Palmolive from O'Sullivan's down Amberley Road.

Nursery Days

Being pushed in a pram by one of my brothers is my very first memory. I would have been be about three. I was being taken to my first Nursery school. This was situated at Carbrook Vicarage on Freeston Place just off Leigh Street and the year 1950. This was because Mum had gone into hospital and my elder brothers were seeing to things at home and making sure every one else got off to school. They said their teachers at school (Coleridge Boys') knew about our domestic arrangements and were very understanding. This day nursery was government run and closed when the new nursery in Carbrook Rec opened in 1951. Now released from its wartime us it was renamed Carbrook Church House and was used to accommodate unmarried clergy and other church workers in the newly formed Attercliffe Parishes. It had a large sitting room upstairs where I played with perhaps half a dozen other children. I used to look out through the big bay windows on to the Hill Top graveyard below and the busy Common beyond. There were many nursery schools in Attercliffe both during and after the war.

Getting women back to work was a priority for the government. Women with children of school age were 'directed' to jobs which meant they had to take them. Only pregnant and nursing mothers were exempt. Mother was directed to work at Brown Bayley's at the top of Old Hall Road in 1946.

Even if you lived outside the school catchment area places were always found. My eldest sister Mavis went to the nursery at the Attercliffe Church School on Leeds Road, then she moved to Phillimore Road School Nursery. This was because one of our elder brothers was going to Coleridge Road School and they used to drop her off before going in to school themselves. This was a very common occurrence in large families with the elder children playing a very big part in schooling their younger siblings. Other people have similar memories of being taken to school by older brothers and sisters, sometimes at great distances and all on foot; nobody had cars in our district except doctors and the odd shopkeeper.

Breakfast was always a hurried meal at our house on school days. One morning, I remember picking up a piece of turnip and eating it on my way in to nursery school. This was the new one in Carbrook Rec. One of the teachers took this off me and threw it into a bin saying that turnip was only for animals. Fancy saying that to a four-year old! Where were these teachers recruited anyway, Cheltenham Ladies College! They certainly weren't local.

Our House

Our yard was situated at the corner of Amberley Road and Manningham Road. There were four families in our yard plus Archie Rogers and his wife who kept the chip shop in the front of Mr & Mrs Sullivan's house. Mrs Rogers was one of the Flather's who ran other chip shops on the Cliff. The Dunn's were on one side of us, the Hillery's on the other. Altogether we were ten adults, seventeen children, two pigeon cotes, one cat, one dog, half a dozen catfish and a plague of mice. We were a community in itself, and never a bad word between us. Living conditions though were very difficult: nine of us in a two-bedroom house. Mother once asked the council if she could be re-housed, but they said we weren't overcrowded. "Well" mother said, "God bless those who are."

We had a Yorkshire Range in our front room where mother did all the baking and some cooking. She mixed everything in a panchen, a massive mixing bowl; you could have bathed a baby in it. She never had any weighing scales, for every item she used was already in 2lb, 1lb or 1/2lb packets. She could cook anything on that Yorkshire Range: joints, casseroles, pies, any baked items. The secret was where to put them. Hot and fast on the top shelf, slow on the oven bottom, and she'd know just how much coal to put on at the right time. There was only one gas ring in the kitchen to cook on. This was connected to a brass tap on the wall by a length of rubber piping. Whenever the ends became perished there was a terrible smell of gas, so the ends had to be cut off. This could only be done a certain number of times before a new length had to be bought. We used to get ours from the wood yard at the back of The Gate Inn.

I felt more than a little sad when we moved out of that house. I don't know why I felt so attached to what was after all a purpose built slum whose only mod. con. was a brass cold-water tap above a stone slop sink. I think it was because that was the last place we were a complete family and the fact that all of us had such a fantastic time growing up there.

The Rag Yard

The lads had more fun or freedom I should say because they had bikes, and they could go anywhere on them. Sometimes a full day out at Cleethorpes or a half-day at Worksop or more usually on the Snake Paths in Tinsley Park woods. Our lads would save up for their bikes and spares and one way of getting hold of a few shilling was by pinching my clothes and taking them to the rag yard to be weighed in. I still have vivid memories of going up stairs one afternoon in the summer holidays. I was pushed out of the way by our Roger. Shock! Horror! He'd just come out of my bedroom with a bundle of my clothes under his arm. He pushed me out of the way and ran off in the direction of Edward Road. It was a fact of life and no good crying over it. Easy come from the jumble sale and easy go to the rag yard, though I never saw him take any of his clothes to be weighed in. There was something else that used to take place during the summer months. At the weekend, a wagon used to park just outside our house and within seconds it would be full of men and women. Scuffles would often break out between them as to who was there first and who should be on the wagon and who shouldn't. They were then taken to farms in Lincolnshire for the potato picking. It must have been good money because the wagons never went half full.

B.F.P.O.

Our Juddy says we moved the year he was demobbed and he says he was never told a) when we were going to flit and b) where to!! Poor Juddy, there he was stood at the top of Amberley Road with his kit-bag on his shoulder looking into our back yard with every house boarded up. He never did say how he found us. Somebody must have told him. At least we didn't have to sent food parcels to him any longer. When he was stationed in the Middle East I used to help mum pack cardboard boxes with biscuit, cakes and magazines. Mother would always flick through the magazines to see if there was anything he shouldn't be looking at. In one magazine, which was a crime thriller, there was a story, with accompanying sketch, about a man who woke in the night to find someone's head on his dressing table. Now, not wanting to frighten him, given his geographical situation (i.e. stuck in the desert between two warring Semite tribes), with such graphic illustrations, she very carefully cut round the shape of the head with a razor blade. She made a very good job of it, but as I pointed out you could still see what she had censored and it looked more grisly than before. Well she said she couldn't do anything about it now, so on went his name rank and number and the letters B.F.P.O.

Have a Go Joe!

In the corner of our living room, high up on a shelf was the wireless set. In the hey day of radio we'd sit round the fire all busy doing something like knitting or pegging and we'd listen to Wilfred Pickles asking embarrassed contestants on his show, *Are you courting love?* This would always bring a roar of laughter from the audience. After a few questions he would then say *Give 'em the money Mabel.* The contestants would get something like 10/- in prize money. Wilfred Pickles was very popular in the 40's and 50's and during the war he became the first Northern broadcaster to read the news on the Home Service. The B.B.C. used other broadcasters with distinctive voices such as Alvar Liddell and John Snagg to read the news in the belief that if the enemy were to overrun the country then the populace would instantly recognize a collaborator's voice. Another of my favourite programmes was *Top Of The Form*, a school's quiz programme. At the end of the quiz each school had to give a cheer to each other. Our Mavis and I used to have fits of laughter when we heard posh girls from Grammar Schools saying 'Hip-rar, hip-rar, hip-rar.' instead of hip-hip hooray, like we used to say. Weren't we ignorant!!

The 1950's was the Golden Age of radio and the B.B.C. in my opinion has never been able to reproduce such successful shows as *Life With The Lyons, The Bradon Beat, The Huggetts, Hancock's Half Hour (We are not layabouts — we are artists, mush!) The Goon Show and A Life Of Bliss.*

Television had just appeared on the horizon and quite a number of families round our way had a television set in the early fifties.

The first time I saw I.T.V. was at a friend's house at the top of Belmoor. I had called on my friend deliberately early so I could stand in the kitchen and have a look at this wonder and it was there I first saw the *George Burns and Gracie Allen Show.* Do you know that man never changed his routine for over fifty years, but why should he I hear you say. He still did his comic dead-pan monologue with that massive cigar in his mouth with his wife as the stooge. They were brilliant. I saw the parents of this friend walking across the 'bomb site' one Sunday afternoon. (We called any area where houses had been demolished a bomb site). I asked what were her parents doing coming out of the empty houses on Blaco wearing boiler suits and carrying sacks over their shoulders. 'Oh' she answered quite casually, 'they've just been stripping lead out of the old houses.' You know, as your parents do in their spare time. Well I thought that's how they can afford a telly!

Coconuts from Gethin's

Having so many brothers was always hard work. I was always running errands for them. They would sit in the best chairs by the fire with their feet up on the fender as often as not cracking nuts and dropping the shells on the floor. 'Wind t'Gilbert up' or 'Change t' needle' they'd shout and 'Put Hernando's Hideaway on ageyen'.

They often sent me to Nelsons, the newsagent at the bottom on Berkley Road, to fetch Reveille or Reynolds News. Sometimes when our Juddy came home on leave he would spend money on us and treat us to biscuits or fruit. 'Go to Gethin's' he would say. By that time everyone would have bolted out of the house except me so I had to run the errand. Then he'd say 'Go and fetch a pound of broken biscuits and a pound of mixed nuts, but tell Mr Gethin this time we don't want any coconuts in.' I'd only be about five or six and by the time I got to the shop I would say to myself, there wouldn't be any room in the bag for a coconut would there? I never repeated the message.

Years later when I called in Gethin's on my way to school, a new arrival on Kingslake Street came into his shop carrying a bundle of washing. She was going to the newly opened laundarette at the top of Berkley Street, but wanted her bundle weighing before she went. She dropped the dirty clothes into Mr Gethin's arms, pointed to the scales then said 'Weigh". Mr Gethin nearly blew a fuse! He told her his scales were for weighing food and not for her dirty washing!

Whenever my mother sent me on an errand she would say, 'Go to the little house window shop next to Abbott's will you?' or 'Go to the little three steps glass trinket shop near the Gate Yard will you?' It was like running errands for Dylan Thomas. Whenever I was sent to the butchers it was always Thorpe's mid-week with two bob. I would be instructed to put the florin on the counter, let the butcher see it, then say 'Mam wants half a pound of steak' that way he'd know not to go a penny over because he'd know that was all I'd got. On pay-day it was different, it was half a crown and I was to go to Oliver's. Dearer but better, but it still the same performance. Always let the shopkeepers see your money.

D.D.T.

Our Mother used to do a lot of wallpapering for neighbours and I used to go with her to help. We used to make the paste with flour and water. I don't know if this was for economy or because proper paste wasn't available in the shops. White paint wasn't available until I think the late fifties; so all the woodwork was done in mushroom. Bedrooms were always distempered; ours was in a garish orangey-yellow. Distemper was a powder that was mixed with water and applied with a broad brush. Going back to the paste, I think it was the flour in the paste that encouraged bugs. When my mother first went into our 'new' house on Coleridge we had to completely strip the paper off the walls in the front room because mum found dead bugs behind the wall-paper. We had to wash the walls with D.D.T. before we re-papered. The bugs would feed on the paste and the horsehair in the plaster. Mother said she knew people that had nets over their beds so bugs would not drop on them whilst they slept.

The internal walls in the bedrooms were made of laths covered in plaster. They weren't very strong and easily punctured by fist or boot of fighting sons and husbands. It was my job to stuff these holes with sheets of newspaper soaked in paste before mum got to that part of the room.

D.D.T. had been taken off the market for some time but my mother still managed to get hold of the stuff. She had this secret stash that she kept in some old bread bins in the cellar. She would sprinkle it around the perimeter of the kitchen and in the shoe cupboard. Whenever you went for your shoes you would have to bang them on the floor then turn them upside down. That way, anything inside would come scuttling out then you would clout it with the shoe. I don't know what was more revolting; knowing there was a black-clock in my shoe or having to splatter it all over the lino – Urrgh!!! We did have a real tragedy though. Our cat Sooty lay in the stuff when she went to sleep in the hearth one night. The poor thing got some powder on her and she poisoned herself when she licked her fur. She was found in the morning as stiff as a board. I saw Mother with tears in her eyes as she wrapped her in one of the lad's

old jumpers then give Billy Standish a half-crown to take her to the cats' shelter at the back of the Conservative Club. On warm Summer days folk used to take a chair out side and watch the world go by. Mother was out on a chair one day knitting and talking to passers by when Michael Sullivan our old neighbour from Manningham Road came walking up Coleridge Road. He had just been to the Sally to fetch ale for the men who had been tapping the furnaces at Brown Bayley's. It was hot work and this was normal practice. The mashing cans were wedged on the brush stale with nails so they wouldn't slip off and spill their precious contents.

The Pop Shop & Lizzie's Pram.

I once asked mum if she ever went to the pawn shop at the bottom of Berkley Road and she replied very quickly that she had never pawned anything in her life. I don't think that was quite true because thinking back I used to miss certain items of clothing, but it never entered my head to ask where they had gone. I'm thinking in particular of Whitsuntide clothes and the time mother took me to the Co-Op Drapery Dept at Kirkbridge Road. Do you remember that shop, it had leaded lights in all of its windows with the words 'mantles', 'capes' and 'gowns' picked out in black. If I may jump a few years here I have a particular fond memory of this department because upstairs were the Co-Op Check Offices and it was here that my sister Mavis got me my first job.

As a junior I had to serve tea and sandwiches to all the staff at their mid-morning break. I was particularly amused when the 'cook' and I use the term loosely here because I never saw her make anything except bread and dripping sandwiches and the odd scone. Well, she told me to go out and fetch three loaves for that morning's breakfasts. 'Don't go to the Grocery Dept downstairs.' She whispered, ' Go to the corner shop on Old Hall Road. They sell Gillots! And don't let Sam Oliver (The Manager) see you!' What an advertisement for Co-Op bread!

Well to get back to the story, mother bought me a beautiful yellow Rayon dress and brown blazer one Whitsuntide, but I don't remember wearing them after the holiday. I wouldn't be surprised if they had been sold. I don't know how mother coped, kitting us all out on these special occasions. Then she let drop that her friend and neighbour in the next yard, Lizzie Rowbotham, used to push a pram up Manningham Road on Monday mornings, collecting parcels which she would then take to the Pawn shop. I bet that's where our stuff ended up – in Lizzie's pram.

Carbrook Play Centre

Winter nights were never dull. We used to go back to school after tea to the Play Centre. This was held in Carbrook County Junior School main hall and in the classrooms around it. A few teachers would stay behind and give dancing lessons to the girls, and the boys would do basket weaving. I always though it was decent of them to give up their spare time to entertain hundreds of kids who otherwise would have had nothing to do during the long winter nights. So belated thanks to George Neal, Granville Twigg and 'Pop' Naylor and Mesdames Gillott, Featherstone and Renshaw. Excuse my memory for they may be others.

The lads would make everything from jam-jar holders to fishing baskets and I used to love watching the girls doing the 'Polly Glide' all with their arms linked, singing….'Take a boy like you, Take a girl like me…' All moving in perfect harmony with each other and full of confidence. They were my sister's generation and I thought they were fantastic role models. I was too young to join in but loved to stand at the door and watch them.

Our Mavis used to go to the youth club at Coleridge Road School and she was forever ironing the same black skirt every tea-time. She used to brush this stuff on it called Thawpit. It stank to high heavens. It was a sort of solvent, the same stuff that dry-cleaners used. She would then iron it underneath a sheet of brown paper so it wouldn't get shiny. The irons were kept on the open fire grate and, to make sure they were hot enough, you would have to spit on them. If the spit shot off like a bullet out of a gun then you knew the temperature was right!! All scientific this you know and if she wasn't ironing her only black skirt then she'd be sat with her head glued to the pages of Red Star or Red Letter. Cheap romances, they were printed on rough War Time economy paper with print that had to be read within 24 hours of publication otherwise it would fade away

before your very eyes! We used to get our comics from kids who knocked on the door asking if you had any to swap. There would be a frantic rush around the backs of chairs and settees and under cushions to find comics that were finished with, but too good to chuck out, and kept for such occasions: Swap Time. That's when we got to read the posher end of the comic market. We had the Dandy and Beano delivered, but this way we got hold of Eagle, Girl, Superman, Batman and Frankenstein. These had glossy covers and were special.

The street games we played in summer were Kick-Can, British Bulldog, Finger Thumb and Rusty Bum. There were also Dares. This was where friends would dare each other to run up someones entry and climb over the wall into someone else's yard on the next street. Bad luck if the yards were on two different levels, you could end up with a badly sprained ankle or be chased by someone coming out of a back door or closet. The rule was if you didn't live up that yard, then you'd no business being up there and if you got caught you'd get a scutch.

There was one area though where we never played and that was at the very top of Manningham Road by the Rec. railings. Here on the right hand side was a disused, rusted up gate that led up to the old Co-Op Garages. This building was used as a temporary mortuary during The Blitz. Mother said she remembered seeing ambulances going up there. Now I never knew that until recently, but that area was always out of bounds to us as kids. Nobody told us about it, we just felt it was somehow spooky and I've heard others say the same thing.

Flittin' & Feytin'

In the mid-fifties, Brown Bayley's moved everyone off Manningham and Blaco Roads in order to extend their East Forge. Our 'new' house was just a few yards round the corner on Coleridge Road between Glave Street and Swan Street. We carted everything ourselves. The kids pushed small items in the wheel-barrow and the men did the heavy jobs: dismantling the bedsteads and rolling up the palliasses. A palliasse was a poor man's mattress; there were no springs in them. It was something like a duvet-cover but made out of strong grey and white ticking. It was filled with flock, waste from the Cotton Mills and was stuffed tightly and sewn up at the end. (out-workers in the Lancashire towns made them, and a source of extra income for women there. They'd get a shilling for stuffing and sewing each one.) If you were lucky you got two to sleep on. If not, you got one. I had one and it was full of lumps. My mother said that when she was a child growing on Catley Road, Darnall, they didn't even have these. Theirs were filled with chaff, which they got from the farm further up Catley Road in the woods. This was because there were so many children and babies in the house they had to refill them so often until the little ones were dry at night.

Nobody ever told us we were poor or that we never had any luxuries in life. I'm glad I didn't know. But if we were poor materially then we had the best in terms of a happy family and strong relationships. We did argue and fight though; I must say this to balance the picture. This was because I was a bit of a tom-boy who would answer back. I remember one occasion when one of my brothers chased me across the yard. I managed to get in the lav just in time and I had the foresight to remove the sneck from the latch before slamming the door shut. That way he couldn't open it. He said he would wait all day for me to come out then he would bash me, so I stood on the lav seat and reached into the cistern and held down the ball cock. This in turn let in more water than the cistern could hold and the excess went gushing out through the overflow pipe that was directly over my brother's head. He got the gush right on top of his new crew cut! I cannot recount the number of times he was beastly to me because there isn't room to list everything! I will though tell you what happened when he first came home with his new crew cut. He walked in the kitchen, took his monkey cap off, looked in the mirror above the mantlepiece then started

wrourin!! Then he ran up to his bedroom and slammed the door – they had cut his quiff off – his pride and joy! It was goodbye Bill Hayley, hello G.I. Blues!!

When we flitted to 28 Coleridge Road, we called it our 'new' house but in fact it was a good thirty years older than the one we left. Mother had only a few days in which to get the house ready to move into. Together we painted and decorated the two downstairs rooms and whitewashed the closet in the back yard. The new house did have an extra bedroom that we sorely needed: an attic bedroom, it had no lighting so our brothers gallantly said we, my sister Mavis and I could have it.

I noticed this was something regular round our way. Sons got all the best. I even knew of one school friend who slept in the front room on the settee at night and her brother slept in the only spare bedroom. Some years later I was to ask mother why she moved from one small cramped house to another, when Mrs Dunn our neighbour on Manningham Road had moved to a very well proportioned house. It had three bedrooms and I think an attic, a slop kitchen and a garden on Howden Road and they only had three children. Well! She argued Mrs Dunn had to pay 10/- a week more for her house. We were paying 16/9 for our house on Coleridge Rd by the time we left in

1971. I've always wondered just what Mrs Dunn was paying in the late fifties. I bet it was less than a pound. We should have had a house like that, but I suppose mother thought that as the eldest two were on the threshold of getting married and moving out, time would ease the pressure.

The home environment I grew up in was one that would have been familiar to my grandparents, yet to my children totally alien. They look at me in amazement when I tell them of the times mother would make a fire in the bedroom whenever one of us was ill. They can't imagine a bedroom with an open fireplace in it!

In our house on Coleridge Road, there were no electric plug sockets. The first electric irons we had were plugged in to the light sockets, as was the wireless. When we eventually got a T.V. in 1959, Dad paid an electrician £5 to install two sockets before we could plug the thing in. There was no hot water on tap, no central heating and no one had a telephone. What a seismic shift in living standards, but we survived those days and I think we are the better for it. Certainly I think the semi I live in with all its mod cons as little short of Heaven.

Supermac & The Good Times

The early fifties brought a little economic boom to our house. All over the place, Army Surplus shops were springing up. Most of the stuff in our house was second hand or handed down from grandparents. I remember helping our Brian and Mavis push a leather Chaise-lounge up Steadfast Street in the dark. It cost 2/6d off Mrs Gregg. Now we had new cutlery, pots and pans and bedding from these shops. I must say, though, that our Mother never bought anything on credit. Major items like beds and sofas were bought from The Cosy Furnishing Co. near Carltonville Road. There you had to pay for things weekly and when they were fully paid for they were delivered.

To keep warm on bitterly cold nights, mother used to take the plates out of the oven and wrap them in old jumpers to keep our feet warm and cover the bed with overcoats. Now we had brand new woollen army blankets: grey with a red stripe border. Oh! The sheer luxury of it. To feel the rough male kiss of warm woollen blankets, if one may get poetic about it!! Men also bought their clothes from these shops and to watch them going to work was like watching a platoon of squaddies on the march. It was khaki everywhere you looked. Khaki blouses, khaki trousers, khaki shirts, caps and scarves very likely khaki underwear too. My brother and I once went to the ironmonger's shop at the top of Steadfast Street, which was full of Army surplus supplies. For 1/6d Martin got a pair of pilot's goggles and I went walking around with a flight navigator map case strapped to my leg! You don't care when you're ten do you?

In the world of fashion we had the post-war New Look by Christian Dior in 1947 and though the London scene had a new verve during this period it took some years to reach the provinces. You would not have seen women on The Common in the haute couture of the London fashion houses, but with the help of Dubarry's, mid-fifties women were wearing some very smart outfits. I can't go without mentioning our men and how they dressed for a night out. My brothers went to the best bespoke tailors in Sheffield: Barney Goodman and they stopped the traffic whenever they walked out of the front door!

So the dark days of post-war austerity and rationing were behind us and by the late 1950's, everybody became home conscious. Everywhere, front doors were being flushed, glazed and painted by the score. Out went bottle green and chocolate brown and in came sky blue and canary yellow. Suddenly it was a technicolour world. Full employment, strong trade unions and access to hire purchase were the reason I suppose. What did Harold MacMillan say during his re-election speech in 1959? 'You've never had it so good.' How right he was!!

Poes, Pots & Chambers

Another facility which we, and everyone else, lacked was an indoor toilet, and like everyone else we had something to use in the night. This was an enamel bucket that was a quarter filled with cold water and disinfectant and put out on the landing each night. Those who came home full of beer would keep everyone awake all night pissing it away and I'll never forget one morning when some inconsiderate user put the bucket right at the bottom of the stairs to my room. In my rush downstairs on a dark winter's morning, my foot found the bucket and its contents before it found the floor. After filling my new black fur lined Chelsea boots (Langtons 50/-) with water and bleach, I then stuck my foot under the tap and poured bleach over it too. I was late for school that morning.

An amusing story that springs to mind here is about a neighbour we had who lived directly across the road from us. Mrs Potts was from southern Ireland and she always had a house

50

full of Irish lodgers and they imbibed, frequently, like every night. Fighting drunk is a term I'm sure was penned for them. One disgruntled ex-lodger was forever coming back to his old abode after chucking-out time. Blind drunk, he would sit on our window-sill and shout 'Come out and fight the two of us.' Now either his arithmetic was all wrong or he genuinely believed the poker he was carrying was actually a drinking friend. Anyway during one drunken brawl, one of them was killed and the police spent a lot of time interviewing Mrs Potts. One evening they were outside her house knocking on the door, but she wouldn't open it. Then they started shouting 'Come on out Mrs Chambers we know you're in there.'
'Why are they calling her Mrs Chambers mother?' I whispered in my naivety. ' Everyone knows her name is Mrs Potts'. Do you know that particular penny didn't drop for many years.

Street Theatre

Another neighbour on Coleridge who was a regular at the Pavilion Bingo Club, was persuaded by her son to join him in Rhodesia in 1962. She bade a tearful farewell to all her fellow bingo pals on her last night on The Common. Hugs and kisses were exchanged and the manager presented her with a bouquet of beautiful flowers. She duly packed her bags and went to the airport. However, seven days later she was back in her seat to the astonishment of all around. They asked what she was doing there; they couldn't believe their eyes. Had she emigrated or not!
'Not stopping there' she growled, 'the place is like a bloody oven and full of darkies.'
Our Curate once made the remark that working class people settled their differences on the street, face to face, unlike middle class people who sent each other solicitors' letters. He made these comments after witnessing an argument between two women on Coleridge Road one Sunday evening as he was making his way to Evensong at St Alban's from Carbrook Church House. I remember the occasion well. It was between Lily, an old neighbour off Manningham and one time buffer girl who worked at the Monogram on Liverpool Street (the only cutlery firm this side of Sheffield) and her next-door neighbour. Now Lily wasn't the sort of person who was backward at coming forward. She was an upfront person, but not as I recall quick to temper or anything like that. Well, on this occasion, she was having a right up and a downer with Mucky Edith and half the street was out to take part in the spectacle. Lily had her arm in a pot at the time and was waving it about to great dramatic effect. This was true open-air theatre. I never knew what started it or what finished it, but it provided a great deal of entertainment for all present.
Other occasions I must say weren't so benign. In fact, they were rather sinister and had the potential for violence. I'm referring to an incident when the man of the house walked out into the road one afternoon in his vest and braces.
He then started to wave his fists in the air and directed his threats to every passer by and those who came out on their doorsteps to listen.
The upshot of his complaint was that people had been talking about him and his family, saying his youngest child was not his. The child was dark because she was a 'throwback', he remonstrated, and if any body said different then they would get this. A tightly packed fist was then shown to all present. All the while, his wife who was seated in the doorway started dabbing her eyes, distressed that anyone could doubt her fidelity. A very clever woman, she had flirted with danger in the most remarkably way possible by reporting the gossip to her violent husband and thereby pulling off a most remarkable coup. Innocent of all charges M'Lord!

Cardboard Kalashnikovs

The year was 1959. I remember because it was the year the Cuban Revolution came to Attercliffe one sleepy Saturday afternoon. Most Saturdays I called at a few shops for my brothers buying boot seggs at one and a jar of Brylcreem at the other. I always went to Woolworth's further up the Cliffe for their paper collars. I never bought much for myself there, but the day was never complete unless I'd had a walk round. By the back door to Zion Lane was where the light bulbs were displayed and on the right of the door was the mouse trap counter. I could never walk past that display without seeing if I could prime one; which I always could, but the tricky bit came when I had to dismantle it without it taking the end of my thumb off. What the assistant on the bulb counter thought I was doing every week-end at this counter I'll never know. Perhaps she thought in a perverse sort of way I was enjoying myself. For me it was a mental exercise, should I let the bait tray loose first or should I just throw the thing down and hope I could get my hand out of the way in time. These are the things that occupied the mind of a 12 year old on a Saturday with nothing else to do. It was while I was contemplating life without my left thumb that a commotion broke out at the front of the shop. There were half a dozen women, all with their hair in curlers, screaming with laughter and the shop assistants behind their counters were frozen with disbelief. The cause of the astonishment and merriment were four young men all dressed as Fidel Castro complete with long hair, berets, flack jackets and cardboard cut outs of rifles and pop guns. They had just burst in the front doors and had began persuading everyone to put donations in their collecting tins. They were Raggers and like all good revolutionaries had broken off from the conventions of the University Students Rag Parade in the city centre, jumped on a tram and taken the revolution to the suburbs. It was the most exiting thing I had ever seen in my life. Not only had these young educated middle class men brought an event that had taken place in the outside world into our closed isolated one, but they had put us all centre stage by re-enacting the event in the heart of our village for our benefit. It was street theatre at its best and made me in particular feel elated at having witnessed something so important. I wonder if those students ever thought what effect their hilarious antics had on one juvenile shopper that Saturday in 1959.

The House of Fools

For every bright spark, there was a houseful of fools and we in our time on The Common had known our share of them. One family we knew bought a dog that they named Rover. Nothing strange in that I hear you say, except this dog happened to be a bitch, so we called it Rovena. Anyway, one day Violet came up our back yard with her dog which happened to be a lot smarter than our neighbours because he knew the dog was a bitch and what's more the bitch was in season. Pandemonium ensued for about half an hour while the distressed owners of Rover/Rovena tried to get the visiting dog off its back. It was only after three buckets of cold water had been thrown over the pair that both dogs were separated. Violet said it wasn't her fault because any bitch in season should have been kept indoors. What puzzled me though was the fact that not one person in that household knew that boy dogs had trantlements between their legs and lady dogs didn't.

This same woman came to see mother a few months later with a matinee jacket she was knitting for pending arrival. Something wasn't right she said showing said garment to mother. Mother took it off the needles and said 'Unless your baby is going to have three arms we don't need a third sleeve do we?' She then unravelled it all and started her off again. I was behind the kitchen door giggling.

In my beginning is my end.

Looking back, I have nothing but happy memories growing up with my six brothers and sisters and many school friends. As children, we were never assaulted and we never assaulted anyone. None of my class-mates ever stabbed anyone, and I never heard of any thirteen-year old girl getting pregnant. We were never burgled and we never played truant and yes we could go out and leave our doors unlocked, and a bang with the rake on the fire-back would bring the next-door neighbour in for a cup of tea. These are not rose-tinted images from the past: they are fact. What went wrong then, and why was poor housing seen as enough reason to destroy a community that was on the whole law abiding and not afraid of hard work?

Of course we needed new homes and yes it would have been nice to have all the things that made life more comfortable like bathrooms and central heating. However, we could have been re-housed street by street and our community could have continued. It was as if the old Anatomy Act had been revisited upon the poor but this time upon the body corporate. We were now at the mercy of every greenhorn town developer and architect who was allowed to practice his or her skills on the dying district.

It was only in the 1980's when I watched the destruction of the mining industry and the pit villages that I realized 'I'd sat through this movie before'. Its money that matters and not people, and if profits in certain industries start to fall for whatever reason then the sooner the individual realizes he or she matters not a jot to those who make the laws in this land then the

better. Our very existence was tied up with the steelworks and their dependant industries: they sank, then so did we. People were treated as movable stock, but if all this had happened ten years later than it did, they wouldn't have found such a compliant work force. Our parent's generation hadn't learned to organise themselves and there was still a culture of deference to those 'who knew best'. But just remember this, if you came from the East End then you came from the Best End and whatever becomes of our 'Village' in the future, it is still part of us. No one can take from us that which they cannot possess – our memories and our experiences. So tell your grandchildren about your life and schooling in the hey day of Attercliffe. Posterity will thank you.

A Family Album

Elsie Hillery, Ann Hillery and Jennie Sapcote 1949

When we look at past pictures of all those we shared

Our lives and dreams, our hopes, our cares.

Cherish the memories and keep to your mind,

Love's shadows and whispers on the great Path of Time.

A.S.

Ann & Roger Sapcote 1948

Martin Sapcote on manoeuvres in our back yard 1953.
He's wearing his Air Raid Warden's tin hat.

Della, cousin of the Hillery's. That's our mangle under the
rug spoiling the shot. Sorry Della!

Jimmy Dunn & Ann Sapcote 1950

Roger Sapcote with bow and arrow ready for the
German counter offensive in our back yard 1952.

Bill & Elsie Hillery hosing everyone down during the hot summer of 1953. The kids are left to right:- Ann Hillery, Irene Dunn, Ann Sapcote, Marion Dunn and Cynthia Hillery

left: Mum with daughter Ann and Marion Dunn from next door about 1950. Over the wall lived Dave & Lizzie Rowbotham, The Harrisons & The Moats. Edward Road is in the background showing the garrett- high houses of the block under study in the chapter 'Workmen's Cottages'

above: Nursery furniture was always passed on to whoever needed it. The infant's chair and table could be converted into a high chair as well. I remember our Jenny using it in '55. Making use of it in this shot in 1949 is I think Marion Dunn. Is that her brother Jimmy? Here we have a good view of the slop kitchen at the back of Mr & Mrs Sullivan's house. They were called slop kitchens because the sinks in them were called slop sinks. Not to be confused with slop-buckets or slopping out. Slop buckets were taken to the closets first thing and the contents flushed away.

This photograph was taken at the very top of Amberley Road. We had all gone round to Anne Robinson's to play at Weddings with her friend Sadie Taylor who lived at 8 Blaco Road. We are right to left:- Ann Sapcote, Sadie Taylor, Marion Dunn, Anne Robinson, Ann Hillery and Cynthia Hilery.

Birthday Party for Ann Hillery in our back yard 1954. Around the table left to right are:- Cynthia Hillery, Ann Sapcote,?, Christine Gregg, Ann Hillery, Linda Gambon, ?, Marion Dunn, Sadie Taylor.

Mavis Sapcote aged 12 outside Mrs Dunn's house 19 Manningham Road.

Mavis, top row right taken at Thornberry Annex, Ash House, Dore. Mavis spent 13 months there recovering from Rheumatic Fever. In all she lost two years at Coleridge Road School. When she returned to school she was made Head Girl.

Mum & Violet used to take bags of toffee for all the kids on the ward when they went to visit. They would scan the evening paper to see what ward new patients were on and who was on the isolation ward. House parties were always held for kids who had recovered from Scarlet Fever and other such life threatening illnesses.

On the left is Martin Sapcote aged 3. In front of the group is Michael Moats who lived in the next yard. Just on the edge peeking is A. S. and in the kitchen doorway, brother Brian can just be seen getting washed off in the kitchen.

Ann & Cynthia are at the back.

The Sapcote's and the Dunn's take a break to have their happy days recorded.

Keith Hillery with his new bike. It must be wash-day because everyone has taken up their rugs and thrown them on the wall. Over the wall Mrs Turner & Mrs Robinson have their back doors open.

Here are the usual crowd standing at Mrs Sullivan's back door. Jean Smith is here at the front on the right. Jean lived on Berkley Road.
This was the last summer before we flitted in 1956.

Cynthia with her pram and a view of the top of Amberley Road

Younger sister Jenny at Jean Gregg's Wedding in 1958.

Violet's son John Gregg in 1955

Outside The Vulcan Inn, Sussex Street, Norfolk Bridge 1951.
To be correct the house next door where our cousin Joan's Wedding Reception was held.
Left to Right:-Edith Sapcote, Rita Standish, Jennie Sapcote, Isabel Sapcote, Lily Sapcote- Outram, Uncle Eric's sisters and cousin Audrey Outram at the back.

Dad & neighbour Tommy Dunn 1949

A rare indoor shot of our Dad reading the latest on the war in Korea. c.1953. You can read the actual headlines, Infantry at Truce.

Shot in the kitchen of 17 Manningham Road, Dad is sitting by the fender. Not bad for a simple Brownie Box camera. The décor was dark brown varnish over a sort of anaglypta with orange and green fan design above the border.

We got all our wallpaper from the Co-Op at the top of Berkley Street. Every roll had to have the edge trimmed off. Later the edges were perforated so a hefty whack on the fender rail would knock it off. Trimming paper was nearly as boring as winding an ounce of wool into a ball. The fender was bought for five bob from someone on Manningham who worked at Brown Bayley's and was making them at work on the quiet.

Left: Our Mama, Jennie Brown age 18. She was brought up by her loving Aunt Agnes and Alice & Liza Brown of Catley Road, Darnall. Beloved mother of seven, we adored her. She was strict with her girls though. 'In at nine and no Laddin' she'd say as we went out.

Brothers Brian & Roger 1968.

Mavis in 1954 at the entry to Jean Gregg's yard at 31 Coleridge Road. Mavis is wearing a silky black and white check dress from C&A and black suede ballerina slippers.

Left: Aunt Gladys and Uncle Joe Sapcote (back row right) at Tony and Pat's Wedding 1971. Young Joe is on the right.

Joe lived on St. Charles Street down Oakes Green, a tall strong man he fell into a casting pit when he was on the night shift at the Brightside Foundry and broke his hip. This left him with a limp all his life but the compensation he got led to a year long party usually starting in the Dog and Partridge he would carry on till he'd been in every pub on the Cliffe. Aunt Gladys did get her fur coat though.

Mother in Miss Carr's garden in 1962.

Mother worked for Miss Carr, the Headmistress at Carbrook County Infants School for three decades as a daily help and companion. After mum had finished her jobs they would have dinner together. Miss Carr retired at the age of 65 in 1962 and spent most of her holidays in Scotland with her family. Miss Carr died in 1973 at her cousins' home in Sutherlandshire.

332 Coleridge Road in my sister's yard at the corner of Century Street and Coleridge Road. I used to love walking up Coleridge to visit my sister and thought her house and its positioning really nice, it always seemed to catch the sun up there. The homes were really nice too. They had two bedrooms and a small one over the off shot kitchen. The lads round there were really cheeky though. One evening when our Mave was washing the pots she thought she heard something outside in the yard but thought nothing of it until she went out the following morning to fetch the milk in. Some cheeky sods had sawn away everyone's lead waste pipes from under their kitchen windows! No doubt they got a good price at the scrap yard next door! I'm holding my nieces Rachael and Helen and standing in her doorway is Mrs Simpson. Do you see the dip in the sandstone window- sill in the photo below? That was the result of years of sharpening the carving knife on it every Sunday morning.

Martin Sapcote with friend Richard Martin who came off Thurley Place. 1965.

Martin and Richard both went to Grammar school after attending Carbrook County Juniors and went to the youth club on Woodburn Road.

Coleridge Road Boy's School Class 3c 1957

Back Row left to right: no.3 Joe Webster, no.6 ? Brooks, no. 7 Mick Gill, no. 8 ? Ford.

Middle Row: no 1 Paul Glossop, no. 2 Fred Welbourn, no. 3 Roger O'Brian, no. 4 Mick Bradly, no. 5 Morris Peaker, no. 7 Leslie Callaghan, no. 8 ? Schofield. Front Row: no.1 Khan, no. 2 David Wood, no.3 John Gregg, no.4 Graham Roddis, No. 5 Michael Housham, no.6. Jack Stevenson, no.7 Leslie Walker.

The Wednesday Shield 1957 Coleridge Boys 3 Wisewood School 1

Back Row Left to Right:- Mr Stribley, Alan Dransfield, Mike Smith, Derek Paris, Dave Richardson, Dave Blackburn, Roger Sapcote, Alan Jones, Sports Master.

Front Row Left to Right:- Len Badger (later to play for Sheffield United), Pete Wragg, Rod Burnham, Pete Barrett, Vic Sheldon, Jimmy Bayliss.

Elaine Morgan and P.T.Class in the Boys Yard Coleridge Road School 1951.

In the background is the Science Annex and top Coleridge with the junction of Century Street on the right.

Coleridge Girls' School – Miss Dickman, Head Girl & Prefects 1954

Back Row left to right:- G.Clakell, Pat Bennett, Enid Burke, M.Gutteridge, Pat Flinton, Doreen Burford.

Front Row:- S.Thompson, Joyce Green, Mavis Sapcote, Miss Dickman, Anne Stuart, Kathleen Thompson, Beryl Burgess.

Jessop's & The Real Giants of Steel

OUTSIDE THE LIGHT FORGE ON WEEDON STREET
From Left to Right: – Ernest Charlesworth, Cliff Tantum, Stan Wray, Judd Sapcote. c.1968.
Note the sweat towels and leather aprons: the badge of their trade.

Our Dad, George Edwin Sapcote, son of George Wilson Sapcote and Elizabeth Ann Barber (Manchester) and grandson of Isaac Abraham Sapcote and Isabel Miller, daughter of George Miller, spring knife maker and publican of the Cutlers Arms, Worksop Road. Here he is, first on the right, pictured outside the light forge at Jessop Saville's, Brightside. Dad looks about 60 in this photograph, so I guess the year would be 1968. His was a very hard and exacting job and he worked at the forge from the age of fifteen until he retired at 65. I never really knew just how hard his job was until last year when I was invited to look round a forge on Tinsley Park Road courtesy of the manager Mr Terry Hibberson. Terry used to be deputy manager at Jessop's and knew my dad all his working life from 1955 when he started as a shop floor worker earning 30/- a week. Terry was promoted to Deputy Manager and worked there until the firm closed.

When I first walked into the forge I turned right round again and walked out! Terry grabbed me by the arm and said not to be frightened and that it was quite safe where we were. He then walked me over to a 28cwt hammer and said ' This is what your Dad did all his working life.' I could hardly keep back the tears. How could anybody do work like this and remain sane. What stress this must have put on all his joints and muscles. No wonder he suffered with a bad back and sore feet all his life. You had to be a Titan to be able to manipulate those giant tongues and pull the white-hot rings out of the furnace and carry them over to the hammer.

He then introduced me to the man who dropped the hammer over a stamping to demonstrate how it worked. There was a deafening thud and no sooner had the hammer lifted then another white-hot blank was in its place and the process repeated. Terry said all the men he knew that worked at the forge had to have brains as well as brawn as the forging of rings, billets, bars and cranks was a skilled job. The skill was in knowing when and where to drop the hammer, because a drop in the wrong place would produce a crack and that stamping would have to go back in the furnace to be melted again. If a crankshaft was hit in the wrong place then it would disintegrate and the flying shrapnel would have killed everyone in the team. So Terry wasn't exaggerating when he said those men had to have their wits about them. As you can see from the photographs all the men were tall and strong and that got me talking about the men of their day, who were heavy drinkers and not averse to the odd scrap now and then, which in my dad's day meant every other man.

Terry said our dad was a gentle giant but at the same time there was no man at Jessop's who would dare 'cross' him. It was then I told him about the time my dad got into a fight outside The Tram Car. I don't tell this story because I'm proud of it, but rather because it happened and because that was what men were like in those days.

...Dad was drinking in The Golden Ball one evening when a bloke came in and told him three men were smacking his brother Joe outside The Tram Car. Dad left his pint and walked across the road. There was his younger brother sprawled out on the pavement with three men laying into him and giving him a right kicking. Now as it turns out these three men were off duty soldiers. They were young and extremely fit but our dad punched two to the ground so they couldn't get up and the third, he lifted up bodily and threw him through a shop window. An ambulance came for the four injured and dad was question by a C.I.D bloke from Whitworth Lane. There were no charges brought against him because the landlord spoke for him saying he didn't start the fight and he was only looking after his younger brother.

Well that's what happened in Attercliffe in those days. Men used to drink and men used to fight and his dad was a bare-knuckle fighter who used to go into Tinsley Park Woods. It was illegal and there would have been a lot of heavy betting taking place. I also believe granddad used to fight in boxing booths, travelling around with the Fairs in the old days. That's how he met grandma at a Fair in Audenshaw.

When dad went to enlist in the Royal Navy at the outbreak of WWII, they turned him down because he was making gun barrels for them. He did his bit for the war effort in other ways too. He used to fire-watch on the roof of Jessop's and in order to get home during the 'black-out' he would have to feel for the coursey-edge with his hands just to make sure he was on the right side of Janson Street. Mother, however, said he was on his hands and knees because he was blind drunk and couldn't stand up!! Dad would tell us these stories when he'd had a drink and was generally in a good mood. The other major story telling time was on Xmas Eve when he would arrive home early from work pleasantly sociable and with his pockets bulging with spirits. Then he would stand in the doorway and recite *Christmas Day In The Workhouse*. For those of you unfamiliar with this most working class of poems and, in our dad's case, the only poem in his repertoire, then here it is.........

Was Christmas Day in the Workhouse, Behind those white-washed walls.
"A Merry Xmas" said the Doctor, Then someone answered "B***s!"
The Doctor turned round angrily, With thunder on his brow,
"You'll get no Christmas Dinner, You ungrateful little cow!!"

I always think poems such as this were very relevant to people of my parent's age for whom the Workhouse had been an uneasy spectre in their childhood days and relevant at Xmas because they were keeping with the tradition of 12th Night and The Feast of Fools when authority could be mocked. As such they can be described as a piece of working class Saturnian Verse. Well, as rude as it was it made us all laugh and put us all in touch with our dad's lighter side again.

Dad used to get home at 4.30 every tea-time and depending on who was in, Mother or me, we would help him peel off his shirt and singlet which would be stuck to him with sweat. Then we would put out a bowl of water for him to wash. After that he would sit down

Outside the Light Forge are Joe Mackewicz, Ernest Charlesworth and Cliff Tantum. The gate on the right leads on to Weedon Street and the stock-yard across the road by the side of the railway embankment.

and we would take off his boots, socks and bandages and bring a bowl of water for him to put his feet into. While his feet were soaking we would mash tea in a pint pot for him, then we would wash his feet. This was a ritual that was performed every day, all very biblical, but I'm sure it was done in every home.

Our dad was very short tempered and we all had to be very quite when he was at home. He always slept for an hour or two then went out to the pub till closing time. His favourite pub in the 50's was The Filesmith's Arms. Dad earned good money at Jessop's but there were occasions when he was put on short time and had to sign on. Sometimes he would go to the Labour Exchange by the Globe or sometimes if it involved a lot of the workforce, someone would come to the Works and sign every one on en-mass. Whenever Dad drew a short wage, then Mother had to take a drop in housekeeping too. This was a constant source of friction between them. I reckoned Dad was earning between £10-£15 in the fifties but nobody knew for sure because he would never tell anyone, not even mother. I have since been told that he was on £12 per week in 1955, so I wasn't far out.

Dad's brother, Uncle Joe, was a constant source of mirth to us all and we used to roll with laughter at his antics. He was a great leveller and the exact opposite of our Dad. Joe lived on St. Charles Street down Oakes Green, a tall strong man he fell into a casting pit when he was on the night shift at the Brightside Foundry and broke his hip. This left him with a limp all his life. The two thousand he received led to a year long celebration usually starting in the Dog and Partridge. He would carry on till he'd been in every pub on the Cliffe. This was in the late fifties and one afternoon when our Roger had just finished work ripping out old fireplaces nearby he thought he'd call in on Uncle Joe even though he was still in his work clothes and black bright. He was made so welcome but refused a drink on account of him only being fifteen and it was only four in the afternoon, then Uncle Joe opened a cupboard door to reveal a stash of whiskey from ceiling to floor: his retirement present to himself!! Aunt Gladys did get her fur coat though and for himself a suit. I must say this though; he must have been a man who could take his ale because I never saw him drunk. So it you lived around the Oakes Green area of Attercliffe you would have known Joe Sapcote!

Whenever Dad came home in a bad mood he would sling his boots across the kitchen. He did this whenever he'd been fetched out of work by some policeman and taken to Water Lane in order to bail his brother out again! '£15 effing quid' he would say under his breath. When Joe came to Padley Way on the day of Dad's funeral he delivered the most eloquent and touching tribute to his brother and the sadness of the occasion to everyone present; brothers you see, I never realized the bond was so deep.

Dad's lifelong pal was his brother-in-law Eric Outram and when the time came to leave Attercliffe for good, mother said she would like to live near her family on The Manor. Dad though had other ideas and put his football logic into use. What would happen if the buses were to go on strike; how would he get to Hillsborough? No, they would have to flit to Lane Top or Longley where Uncle Eric and Aunt Lil lived. That way he could walk to Hillsborough and call for Eric on the way. So that was settled and they moved to Padley Way on the Stubbin Estate. I've seen Dad mad with rage at having to pay £5 for a season ticket to watch Wednesday. He would sit and curse as he wrote out the postal order but post it he would and every year too. When he got home after a match mother would never put his tea out until he said so. It would be asking for trouble for if she did for I am sure it would have been slung on the fire back if they had lost, such was his passion for the blue and white shirt.

Dad was born on Garth Road just off Staniforth Road, but by the early 30's they had moved to 13 Manningham Road. Dad was a pupil at Huntsman's Gardens and often told me that he and all the other boys used to wear the Eton collar. His first job on leaving school at 14 was at a stable-yard at the corner of Stoke Street and Lovetot Road. I think it must have been his Dad who got him set on there because he had always worked with horses. He was a Steel Works Carter with his own horse and cart and some of the time he was a Rag & Bone Man. He was so good with horses that when other men's horses were sick they used to send for Granddad. My Mother told me that Granddad once took a donkey into his kitchen because it was raining and he didn't want the poor creature to get wet!! Well they were very close to Nature in those days, weren't they?

Dad went to Jessop's at the age of 15 and never worked anywhere else. He died a year into his retirement age 65. He was a broken man and never lived to really enjoy his new-found hobby of gardening which our Roger got him interested in. When he went to get his papers from the Labour Office on his last day, they didn't know anything about it or who he was. Fifty years of continuous labour and they didn't know him. I saw my dad close to tears when he related this story to me.

As kids we could never understand why our dad was nearly always in a bad mood and difficult to live with. Its only when you become an adult yourself and take a battering from life's storms you understand the sacrifices our fathers made when they went out of the door every morning to sweat their guts out and see next to nothing for it at the end of their working lives except poverty and an early grave. In some cases they never came home at all such was the high mortality rate in the steel industry.

I can still see Dad now in my mind's eye. He's sitting by the fire patching his working clothes or cobbling his shoes. He'd look up at me as I was getting ready to go out and he'd say, *'Such is life in all its stages. Men work and women spend their wages'* or maybe it would be a line from his childhood, and he'd sing *'We spend our money like jolly, jolly, sailors and then we work for more.'* I would join in *'We a-round, a-round, a-round, a-round.'*

A strange scene and all a bit surreal now, but on one last note, if there is anything I have to thank my father for in particular, it

is for the love of books and reading. An extremely well read man he was an authority on our Naval History in both the Wars. Father took me to Attercliffe Library every week of my life when I was at home. There I was like some latter day Elizabeth Barrett, walking out with Papa on Saturday mornings in our Sunday Best to spend a couple of hours browsing and choosing our books. This is Dad sunning himself by the backdoor at 28 Coleridge Road. Our table was never sided. As soon as one lot had finished a meal someone else would want one so mother always left the essentials out, *victuals* as dad called them. He had some wonderful phrases. One of them was 'I'm having a scrape so nob'dy come in't kitchen for ten minutes.' What he meant was he was going to have a bath. Another was, 'Don't be liggin' in bed all day'. (Liggin means to lie down in old Yorkshire and legen in German.) When strangers didn't understand him he would say to me 'Thee tell him.' Then I would translate. Our Dad, Bless him.

The Light Forge Jesssop-Saville's Weedon Street 1960

Arthur Longden	Manager
Terry Hibberson	Assistant Manager
Stan Bowles	Weighman
Ronnie Major	Weighman
Len Staniforth	Sawyer
Harry Glossop	Chipper
Ernest Charlesworth	Chainsmith
Stan Wray	Assistant
Billy Proctor	Blacksmith

30CWT Hammer (no. 27)
Cliff Tantum, George Sapcote, Joe Mackewicz, Kenny Bolsover

15CWT Hammer (no. 25)
Jim Kelly, Howard Keeley, Terry Beardshaw, Jim Liversidge

15CWT Hammer (no. 26)
Bob Cross, Walt Dawson, Wilf Lee

15CWT Hammer (no. 21)
Jack Hough, Albert Pass, Bill Davies, Carl Parkin

Down Our Way

Peacetime and life on The Common was starting to get back to normal in the 1950's. The bad times of pre-war Attercliffe were now folklore and the gang wars on Alfred Road were restricted once cellar grates were chained and only removed when the coal-man came. The newly arrived Arabs forged in that highly conservative and closed society of Southern Arabia carried on where they had left off and while they were busy feuding and stabbing each other or harassing school-girls, locals added their two penn'orth to the crime figures with the murder of a prostitute, running a knocking shop for off duty soldiers and generally punching the lights out of each other every Friday night. For the law abiding majority though the good times were just around the corner with full time work and plenty of it and the introduction of higher purchase meant young couples could look forward to getting married and setting up home with new furniture if not new houses, so welcome to post war life on The Common and the rich tapestry that was working class life there.

The Old Coffee House

The black building in the centre of the photograph was originally the Hallamshire Coffee House. When it was first built around 1880 it advertised accommodation for Cyclists, Commercial Travellers and separate rooms for Ladies. In the 1940's it became Webster's Dining Rooms. It was here in 1946 our grandfather died having fallen down the stairs only days after he had been discharged from hospital still suffering from the pneumonia he went in with. Always a man who carried a few bob around with him, his pockets were empty by the time it took his family to run down Amberley Road to see to him.

In 1956 it was bought by one of the first Arabs to come to Attercliffe and became The Continental Café. This is the place where East met West for the first time, where daggers were drawn and the first liaisons between English and Arab were established. It was here that Val G. who worked as a waitress in the tea room of Terry's Lodging House as it was then known, first met her husband Steve Abdulla, an Arab who said he paid for his boat fare to England from The Yemen by selling his grandfather's gun. Val used to say he always told such fanciful stories but I'd like to bet that one was true. Val and Steve lived on Coleridge Road and had three children.

In 1957 the outside walls of the café were faced in yellow tiles like the ones on The Sally and the building was generally smarted up to become Ahmed's Continental Traders. The son of the owner went straight into the fourth year at Carbrook School. He said his name was Shakr, which he said meant sugar. (It really means 'thanks') He was a very popular lad especially with the girls as his gleaming white teeth and colouring gave him a sort of film star look. Sheila's Dad, whose parents kept the fruit shop next to The Pavilion after Garretts moved out, tells me Shakr, or Tony as he is now known still lives nearby at Tinsley. His Dad's shop held a particular fascination for me; there were goods on sale that I'd never seen or heard of before, and who had ever seen Spaghetti in long hard strands, that can't be right I thought, Spaghetti comes in tins, is soft and covered in tomato sauce.

The shop didn't stay open long. I never saw anyone going in, the folk on The Common weren't ready for the culinary delights of the orient just yet.

17 Manningham Road 1953.

I remember the day this picture was taken. We were going into the Rec and Martin was carrying a teddy bear he'd been playing with all morning when some older boys started laughing at him, he got so upset he wouldn't stop crying so I had to take him home. Mother bought us both an ice cream then our Roger took our photo. To our left is the top of Amberley Road and Archie Roger's Fish & Chip shop. On the next corner where the lamp post is, the home of Aunt Lil and Uncle Eric, cousins Joan and Audrey Outram who later moved to Belmoor Road.

On the right dominating the scene is Brown Bayley's East Forge. The big hammer there was worked 24 hours a day and shook everything when it dropped, but the amazing thing was, it never bothered us. The bad smell from the pickling tanks did though. At the very top was Carbrook Recreation ground and when mother wanted any of us she would stand on the front door step and shout 'Ma – vis (or whoever it was) – You're wan – ted.' Her voice would bounce of the works wall all the way up the road then someone else would take up the cry. Some kid in the Rec would then say to you 'Ey up, somebody's shouting thee.' It never failed.

During the war someone opened a shop on Manningham Road or I should say the bedrooms above for soldiers on leave with nowhere to take their lady friends. The knocking shop as it was called was closed by the police and the person concerned was fined for keeping a disorderly house – or helping with the war effort, take your pick and as Tommy Trinder used to say 'Not all war comforts are knitted you know!'

On the right hand side of Manningham Road was Jackman's Persberg Steel Works, a little firm surrounded by the giant Brown Bayley's. On hot summer days the workmen used to roll up the shutters of the workshop and we used to come out of our houses to play then walk across the road to stand and watch them on their little 'toffee hammers' as dad called them. There we were, our noses inches away from the hammer and bar being worked. We could also sit in our front rooms with the doors open and watch them. We never thought about the dangers or health issues, it was just part of our daily lives.

Looking up Coleridge Road 1966

Photograph by kind permission of the
H Ainscough collection

Ann Robinson 41 Swan Street

I can never look at a photo of Coleridge Road without casting my eye over the bottom left corner where the gas lamp was on its corner with Amberley Road without remembering a great character from yesteryear and that was Little Mary and her chip shop. As the shop was built on the corner it took its exact shape and consequently her shop was shaped like a triangle but with the corner rounded off and here was the door. On either side was a window; one facing The Sally and the other Terry's lodging house. The left side was the frying side and the right side the customer's side. I can still see the sign in the window – Apollo Table Waters.

The shop had a bench which came in very handy when little legs got tired of standing in long queues waiting not as you may think for her customers to be served, but for Mary to come out of the Off Licence lobby in The Sally across the road. She would often slip out for a swift half while waiting for her chips to fry and sometimes I would hear a grown up shout, 'Somebody fetch her, t' chips are burning!'

Someone who knew Mary very well was **Ann Robinson Parker** who lived across the way at 41 Swan Street and it is from her pen that this lovely story comes……

………I remember with a smile little Mary Jenkinson. She owned a chip shop at the corner of Coleridge and Amberley. She was a friend of my grandmother and also of John Manley who came off Leigh Street.

Mary was renowned for her chips because they were always white and loaded with grease. On a cold night my husband Jim Parker said that by the time he reached Brown Bayley's gates by Coleridge Road bridge the chips were a solid block of grease, which you could have thrown and broken any window with.

During the Blitz poor old Mary's chip shop got caught with an incendiary bomb and the corner of the shop got clean cut off. The bomb had landed on a gas main and demolished the main wall of the shop. The next morning when we all came out of the air raid shelter what a surprise we all had. Poor old Mary's belongings were all on show, even the bed and the chamber pot, though all were intact. First of all my grandmother wanted to know if both Mary and her husband were all right of course then asked Mary if she had emptied the pot before the wall had come down! To this day I cannot repeat what her answer was!!!

Mary was quite a character and I loved to go in the shop and watch her chopping up the chips. She was not as tall as you saw her in the shop because she used to walk on a duck-board which gave the impression that she was much taller. John Manley's aunt was also tiny and she used to work for Mary in the shop. John's aunt had a nick- name which was 'Pop' Manley. They looked quite comical when they were out together but when they are your grandma's friends you didn't pass any remarks. You see, Grandma was 5' 10" and weighed between 18-20 stone and both Mary and 'Pop' were about 4' 6". They never took any prisoners though and if any of the lads were rude to them about their height they just sloshed them with a wet tea towel or dish-cloth around their face or neck. It may have been the first time they'd had their necks washed in weeks!

Left: Grandma Mary Ellen who played the Zither. Middle: Gt. Aunt Jane. Right: Gt. Aunt Maggie who once had the chip shop on Manningham when her father Gt. Grandad Titterington (seated) lived at no 13 Manningham Road. Photo c.1905, taken at the back of 47 Swan St, behind the Straw Place.

Mary had a habit or so I'm told. She would slip in to The Salutation and would leave a note on the counter of the chip shop telling the customers she'd be back in ten minutes or so… some hope!!! She'd be sat suppin' in the Sally!!

Just before Grandma died, she told me of a story about when they all went to The Amberley one Boxing Day dinner- time. They had all gone to have a good old knees- up or so my Grandma said. On their way back Mary, Gran and Mrs Pop Manley decided to call back to our house and my grandma, who could play the zither very well and had taken it with her to the pub, had given it to Mary to carry. So when Little Mary who was rather the worse for drink, got to the door of our house, she lifted her little legs up over the step and tripped over into our house, followed by Grandma and Mrs Manley, all on top of each other. Poor old Mary, when she finally got up a bit bruised but still smiling, Grandma said " I don't naw wat thar't smiling at, tha's broken t' old Zither!"

My family lived at many addresses in the early 1900's. On Manningham, on Coleridge and even in the cottages built for the Coke Dressers at Low End on Tinsley Park Road, you know the ones by the weighbridge. This photo however was taken in their back yard on Swan Street, the ones that shared a back yard with the hay and straw place. Well just before the first war this building was pulled down and eventually the Pavilion was built on its site, but it was left as a tip for many years. Anyway, in those days many butchers had their own slaughter- houses attached to their shops and one such was Gillott's at the top of Leigh Street.

The butcher had bought a cow that he collected from Broughton Lane station and he drove it down the Common. Well all did not go to plan because the cow bolted when it got to the bottom of Coleridge Road and ran across the tip right into Gt. Granddad's kitchen. It left its calling card then ran back out onto the Common. My, wasn't there a mess to clean up after that episode.

The slaughter house is still there but is now a garage used by Gavin at Turrett's next to the bank and in the back wall can be seen tethering rings. These stories and many more were handed down to me by my mother and grandma. As the only daughter in a house full of women I was often caught ear wiggin' when I shouldn't have been. Well there was so much to take in and the stuff they were talking about was so funny I couldn't resist listening to women's talk. I was often chased down the street for hiding behind the kitchen door when they were all in full flow as it were! Oh, the things they came out with! Do you see Great Granddad in the photo? Well,

Anne Robinson age 12 on Swan Street in 1951. Note the war- time reminder of the household with a stirrup pump.

they were these photographers who used to do the streets, you know, walk up folks' entry and ask if they wanted a photo taking. They were usually cheap ones done on tin plate, but as you can tell this photo is on card and very professional, but Great Granddad could afford it. In fact when he died, a year or so after this was taken, he left all his relatives £20 each so they could have a booze up in his memory.

One day when one of his daughters was dusting the pelmet above the window, a dozen gold sovereigns came flying off all over the place. That, they realized was his secret hiding place!

There were some sad stories they passed on as well though. I was an only child because when my mother was expecting me Dad left home, but worse was to come. When everyone was out one day, he came back with a horse and cart and cleared the house of all their furniture. What a shock that must have been for Mother, but they learned to live with the tragedies as well as laugh at the good times, that was life on the Common with all its ups and downs.

The only real scandal round our way though was the time a bloke who lived on The Square took up with a prostitute called Russian Edna. She was killed in High Hazels Park and he was arrested for it. Not strictly speaking on our patch still it was a scandal at the time.

Leigh Street Baptist Church Attercliffe F.C. 1901.

Ann Robinson's grandfather Alex Minnis is first on the right in the middle row. I think it most likely the pitch they played on was the one behind The Pheasant at Carbrook. Note the coach has placed his bowler hat in the tree and the player next to him seems to think a tie is this season's must.

The Morgan Family 21 Coleridge Road

Elaine Morgan was born in 1938 and along with her Grandma Minnie, mother Viner and cousin Bill, lived at 21 Coleridge Road in the garret high houses on the left as you looked up from the Common. Growing up in extended families was quite normal in those days and nearly everyone had relations living with them even though 'sub-letting' as the rent man called it, was not allowed and where folks had a spare bedroom i.e. in a three bedroom house then quite often two married couples would share that house.

Elaine says theirs was a cosy little house and she was very happy growing up there. However, when Grandma Minnie died in 1953, Elaine was only fifteen and she remembers the coffin being placed on the table in the front room which she found rather upsetting. She also recalls flowers placed on the coffin and petals all over the carpets. This one abiding memory has left her with a strong dislike of flowers.

Here's a nice shot of Elaine on her bike on Coleridge Road with the junction of Swan Street on the left. Elaine is wearing her green school blazer and wasn't she lucky to have a bike! Must have

been a bit bumpy riding it though looking at the cobblestones. At the bottom behind the bus is the run of shops between Leigh Street and Rotherham Street. They were if I remember right, Kirkup's Ironmongers and Paint shop, a double fronted Fruit & Veg shop, then came Gillot's the butchers. In the 60s this became Nur Bros, Nylons & Sock Shop. Just down Leigh Street you can see the spire of Leigh Street Baptist Church built in 1875. The spire had to be taken down about 1959 and I remember watching this as I came home from school on Coleridge bridge. The Baptists had a very good Youth Club and as far as I remember the church stayed open until the late 60s then a wholesale shoe company was built on the site.

In 1955 when Elaine was 17 her mum married and had a son, John (Everett). This is Elaine pictured here in the backyard at her home 21 Coleridge Road with her baby brother. These are the homes under study in the chapter Workmen's Cottages that were built in 1871 and were known as half back or blind back houses. The first photo shows the backs of house numbers 18 and 20 in Edward Road. The families who lived there were Maurice and Marjorie Round with son Terry. Next door lived Joseph and Sarah Fearn. (See the zinc tub hanging by the back door? That was your portable bathroom. We kept ours under a bed!) Other families who lived in this yard were William and Mary Hobson and their children Brian, Valerie and Gilbert. The local midwife Mrs Ducker also lived in this yard. The homes in this photo have a window in the back to give light to the stairs.

This photo taken in the same yard shows the run of houses numbering 2 to 10 on Amberley Road. They don't have any windows in the back. Also notice the brickwork is much cleaner and free of soot. Pictured in the yard is Elaine's cousin Bill who lived with their family at 21 Coleridge Road. Right is Elaine's mum Viner Morgan photographed at the front of their home on Coleridge Road. Viner worked at Kellit's a little firm that made springs on Attercliffe Road at the junction with top Zion Lane. I don't remember this firm but I do remember what replaced it and that was the first purpose built supermarket in Attercliffe: Carline's Cash & Carry. I think the year was 1962.

When Elaine left school she got a job at Haydon-Nylos on Worksop Road and she married Brian Hobson her neighbour from Edward Road who lived over the back from her in 1957. Brian worked as a scaffolder for the P.W.D. and they first met at the Attercliffe Rads. W.M.C.

The Leversidge Family – 72 Edward Road

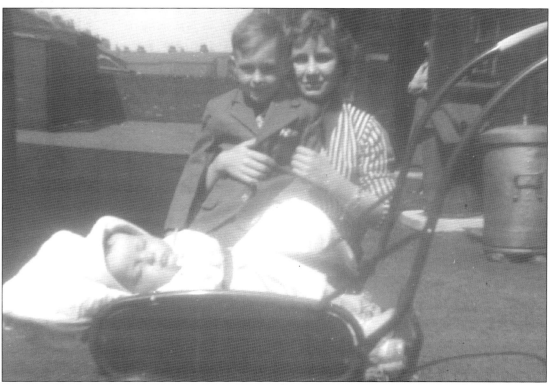

The photo here is of school friend and neighbour Jane Leversidge who with Mum, Dad, sister Anne and brother Peter lived in the top house cornering Edward and Manningham Roads. This photo was taken in their back yard and here you can see the two sides of the lump and the bottom row that faced Amberley Road which were all part of the workmen's cottages built in 1871.

Jane recalls living in a home that was very small with only one room downstairs that served as parlour, dining room and at one time a bedroom for her brother Peter. Above the downstairs room was their parent's bedroom and above that a garret bedroom which she and her sister occupied. When they were all very small, the three children slept in the same bedroom. Jane recalls how spacious it was with room for a single and a 3/4 bed. Their slop kitchen not being off-shot, was much bigger than their neighbours.

In the same yard were two larger houses that faced Manningham Road. They had a large parlour and a large kitchen with three bedrooms. Jane says she vaguely remembers her mum paying 7/6d rent in the 1950s as that was the family allowance for one child, which her mother always put aside for Rent Day. The larger houses just mentioned though were much more, possibly double what they were paying.

In this charming photograph Mrs Leversidge is pictured with her son Peter. This looks like a Butlin's Holiday snapshot.

Violet Gregg 31 Coleridge Road

Violet's mother lived on Liverpool Street when she was born in 1915 but by the time she was 21 and about to get married she was living at no. 6 Berkley Road. Her husband Stanley Gregg lived at 62 Amberley Road and together they moved to Upwell Street at the corner with Carlisle Street East. Perhaps this was near Stanley's place of work; he was a steelworks labourer, but Violet must have felt out of it though because when her husband was called up she moved back on the Common to Belmoor Road. Her husband died of cancer a year after the war ended at the young age of 36. Violet was 32 and a couple of years later she met Ernest Stanton and they became life partners.

 Always on the move Violet flitted to Coleridge Road in 1955 with her children, Jean, Mollie and John. It was there she lost Mollie in a tragic accident. Mollie's dress caught fire and she died a few days later from burns. Some good news though came in 1958; her eldest daughter Jean married regular soldier Bert Tranter and they moved to Bert's home at Fox Hill. Never far from tragedy, Violet lost her brother Charlie Wiltshire a few years later. Charlie had been living at Violet's house on Coleridge Road but for some reason she'd asked him to leave. Charlie had an allotment down Cutty Meadow's. He tried to get to his hut on a cold winter's night but he collapsed on the waste ground just past the last firm on that road and he was found dead in the morning.

In 1962 Violet moved further up Coleridge, over the bridge to the first yard beyond the Scrap Yard. Then she went to live on Clipstone Road and finally to Fife Gardens. She died on the last day in December 1991 from complications that set in after she broke her thigh. A life long wanderer, Violet never had a car and went everywhere on foot or by bus. She'd think nothing of shopping in Barnsley one day then Doncaster the next! And who can forget the sight of Violet in her middle years taking to ride a motor scooter! Complete with siren suit she would put the brakes on and slare her feet all the way down Coleridge Road coming to a gentle stop outside her house, with the soles of her shoes on fire! And the day she won a roll of lino at the Adelphi bingo club. How did she get it home? Well, she stood at the corner of Vicarage Road and flagged down the first lorry she saw! Do you know that bloke took her right outside her home, how's that for charm!

Vi always had the latest gadget in her house. I sat in her house one day having a cup of tea, listening to *Hello Young Lovers*, the hit song from *The King & I.* (to this day I still associate that song with Violet Gregg and her front room on Coleridge Road).

Vi shouted from the kitchen 'Our Ann, plug the Grundig in will you?' I mean, who had a tape recorder in 1957? The plug was under a little table along with a hundred others. I had to try each one in turn in order to find the right one! And for what, just to listen to their John reciting a rude poem about walking by St Paul's when a bloody big bulldog bit his.......Well you know the rest.

Violet wasn't a traditionalist, not for her the staus quo. She went to work and Ernest stayed at home and did the housework, not that he would have gone anyway. Vi accepted him for what he was so Ernest was the first househusband on the Cliffe. She was also the first person I knew who took a holiday abroad, to Dublin by plane, and the first I knew to have a Persian Lamb coat.

Violet was the sort of person who could talk to a stranger and leave them feeling they had known her all her life, and I never heard her say a bad word about anybody. She was also great collector and hoarder which came about I suppose with having such a poor start in life. She had a need to make up for all the years she went without. All the latest gadgets on the market she'd have. Telly, wireless,tape recorder, scooter. She'd have so much wool and material you couldn't get into her front room, and she once sent me upstairs to get a tin of salmon, there was a crate of them on the landing!

I think the funniest story my mum told me about Vi was the one where both of them had just finished work cleaning, up Fulwood way. Mum went to call at the house Vi was working in. It was about three in the afternoon and there was no one about when mother walked up the tree lined gravel drive-way to look in at the kitchen window and see what was keeping her friend. There was Violet by the kitchen sink, sitting over an enamel bucket. After a minute or two Violet emerged totally unconcerned powdering her nose as if nothing had happened. Anyone else caught in flagrante would have never lived it down. No so Violet. 'Well', she explained, ' I'm not running up all them stairs just to have a pee, if a bucket's good enough at home then its good enough round here!' Oh Violet, what a lovely woman you were. This world's a poorer place without you.

Bert Tranter & Jean Gregg's Wedding Day March 1958. Ernest is Best Man. The bridesmaids on the photo's left are Ann Hillery and Della Grayson. Violet is making sure her brother Charlie (white cap) is behaving himself

The Perry Family 14 Berkley Street

The Perry Family moved to no. 14 Berkley Street in August 1939 as war broke out in September. George Perry had been a regular soldier stationed in India and Burma for twenty-two years, and spent all the war years on active service.

Moreen and her sisters recall one neighbour who told them their V.E. Day Union Jack wasn't big enough. Moreen said 'Oh I'll tell me dad when he gets out of that trench he's been in for the last six years to jolly well go and get a bigger one!' Theirs was a two up, two down with an attic bedroom and a bay window. In front there was a paved area originally with iron railings around. These were a better class of home than the ones we lived in on Manningham and Coleridge and definitely at the 'posher' end of the market.

Past their best in the 50's and 60's when I knew the street, there was still the air of the 'shabby genteel' about them. In their prime they would have been a much sought after property, as may be deduced from this photograph of Moreen with her cat 'Monty' on Berkley Street in 1951.

Moreen remembers playing with her dolls and prams in the washhouse in their back yard that was shared with their neighbour.

She says the rent her mum paid in the 60s was 17/6d per week and the rent man found Moreen and Barry a house on Prince of Wales Road in 1963. The rent there was, would you believe, 18/- (90p) per week. Moreen and husband Barry Walker, who was brought up on Phillimore Road, recall many happy days on Berkley and says "We both agree that a tin bath in front of a roaring fire was pure heaven in the days when a bathroom was a luxury and hot water from the tap was just a dream many could only wish for." Note the front doors, they never had a lick of paint from the day they were hung. It was the same with every house on every street. The landlords were too mean to spend a penny more than necessary on maintenance. The tenants quite rightly said it wasn't their job to paint the outside of the house. Why should they increase the value of some one else's property? It was only when D.I.Y. became the vogue in the late 50's and early 60's with such popular T.V. Shows as Barry Bucknall's D.I.Y. programme and the trend in buying ones own home did this attitude change.

Moreen's first job was as a shop assistant at Banner's and together with her work friend they would both go to Attercliffe Slipper Baths on their Thursday afternoon off buying their dinner as they went, they would then sit in a hot bath and eat fish & chips!!! Just picture the scene. I mean, was it a bath- house or a mad- house!! There must have been mushy peas and scraps all over the place. I wonder what the attendants thought of their antics? They probably made allowances for them knowing they were off Berkley.

Moreen recalls doctors blaming many an illness on people having hot baths and then emerging into the cold air. She had a childhood friend, Dorothy Dennison who lived opposite her on Berkley Street, who was thought to have caught rheumatic fever in this way. Dorothy, an only child, was much loved and protected by her parents and the two Miss Whites who occupied the other house in the yard. Moreen spent many happy hours in Dorothy's house listening to her play the piano, saying she had a talent rarely seen amongst youngsters in those days.

Mr Perry and work mate on the 'Cliffe outside Naylor's Jewellers. I wonder if this shop was connected with Naylor's the Pawnbrokers, if so then all our unredeemed pledges must have ended up in their window! The next shop was Betty's. Didn't they sell Wedding Dresses? Then Turner's Drapers and Stylo shoe shop with Woolworth's just out of view.

Right:
Philip Charles Surtees
with friend John Hurst
in the back yard
of the Launderette
about 1953.

Left:
More friends from
Berkley Street. left to right:-
Mary Surtees, Moreen Perry
and Freda Langley

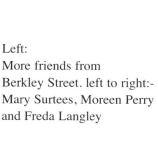

Mr Perry with his daughter Moreen and her friend from next door: Jean Pears. c.1951. The girls are wearing their school uniform of gym-slip and white blouse. They passed their 11 + at Carbrook County and attended Owler Lane Intermediate School.

Mr and Mrs Perry with grandchild and new car. At the top of Berkley Street is the launderette with the offshoot kitchen. That's where the 1d extractor and 6d drying machines were, do you remember going there?

THE MELIA FAMILY 43 BERKLEY ROAD

This is Mum and Dad – Tom & Nellie Melia with my nephew Keith in 1950. Dad worked on the railways and Mum worked as a cleaner. At home were my brothers Tom, Ron, Alf, Ted, my sisters Nellie and Kathleen and me Brenda the youngest.

Our house was at the top of Berkley Road. It was a bay windowed house and had a gable- end as it was the first one in the second run of houses on the left hand side of the road, number 43. We had a living room a back room and a slop kitchen, no bathroom and an outside toilet. We had three bedrooms, the top bedroom had its own staircase so we didn't have to go through our parents' room to get to bed. We never had much money but my, did we have some good times growing up! When we were kids we would play marbles in the street or we would dress up in the back yard and put on a show inviting other kids to watch us. We'd sling a blanket over the washing line and get dressed behind it. Then we'd come out dressed as tramps singing *We're a couple of swells we dine at the best hotels.* After, we would all have a glass of orange juice (6d a bottle from the Welfare Clinic in the Rec.) Under our house was a fresh water stream. Well it was either a stream or permanently fractured mains and we used to chuck pebbles down the cellar steps to listen to them plop in the water. Mother would play hell with us.

In the 1950's all our brothers and other lads on the road were conscripted into the Army or the Air Force and when they were demobbed we would organise street parties for them. We all had a good knees-up on these occasions and I remember Polly Pickersgill who lived further down the road, she had a lovely voice, I thought she was Gracie Fields! Oh what happy times we had and at the end of the day, we'd listen to the lullaby from Brown Bayley's Hammer saying *Good Night Children Everywhere.*

The Melia Sisters in 1950 are left to right Nellie, Brenda & Kath. Taken on Berkley Road with Blaco Road in the background. Ice Sheffield now occupies this site.

We all went to Carbrook County first, then on to Colerdige Road School. I left in 1955 and got my first job at Trickell's, a Cutlery firm on Campo Lane. This is me, aged 17, in my pencil skirt and bolero jacket. I used to buy my clothes from Dubarry's Ladies Fashions on Attercliffe Common. The fashion accessories at this time were bucket bags, vanity cases and plastic popper beads also dirndl skirts were very fashionable. For a laugh, we'd get a hola-hoop, which were all the rage then, and we'd take it in turns to spin it round our waists and try to keep it up by doing the hoola-hoola!

In 1957 I married Jack Holt and we lived in our parents' front room until we got our own house in 1964 at Middlewood and have lived there ever since. We all lived as an extended family of nine when we lived on Berkley Road. It was what we all did, I mean get married and live with your parents until you had enough saved to get a home of your own.

Berkley Road, looking toward the Common, we can see the corner building that was Naylor's Drapery and Pop Shop. On the opposite corner was Nelson's Newsagents. This is our first son Gary taken in 1962 on his third. birthday. Then we had Jacqueline and Gillian in 1960 and 1962. We had our second son Lee at our new house at Middlewood.

Frank Sutcliffe & Family – 79 Coleridge Road (next door to Tom Kirby's shop)

Frank's mum and dad, Frank and Kath, lived on Brinsworth Street and Frank was one of seven children. As he was always close to his Grandma Ada he lived at her house at 79 Coleridge Road. Originally they had a Spice shop over the bridge at 358 Coleridge Road between the scrap yard and Coleridge Place. Then they flitted to the first house over the bridge on the right hand side, a large six roomed house which he shared with Grandma Ada and Grandad Bill Frost who worked across the road in Brown Bayley's No. 6 Mill, Aunt Rosie and cousin Betty. Rosie was a window cleaner and I once saw her clean all the gas lamps on our road in her blueboiler suit and carrying her little pointy-topped ladder.

There were three houses in Frank's yard with the shop-keeper renting two and using the middle house for storage. These were Brewery houses (Duncan Gilmour's) and before Tom Kirby, Tom Bridges had the shop and before that a bloke called Frank. Tom Kirby would sell most things on strap, but if customers fell behind with their payments he would write their names and how much they owed and put it in the window. He was the original 'name and shame' man. One of Tom's business pals was the bloke who ran a little corner shop at the top of Belmoor Road. A newcomer to the district he was upset at not being able to sleep at night because of the noise from the big hammer in the East Forge. The story goes he rang up the Managing Director of Brown Bayley's at his home at Whirlow in the middle of the night and asked him if he had any trouble sleeping! That, folks said was the reason every one was moved out of the district. Was that Dr. Bull's revenge?

Some of the neighbours Frank remembers are Frankie Mincher who had a rag cart which he parked at the yard on Edward Road. When Frankie became head barman at The Sally his pals made a medal for him from a cocoa tin lid which apparently he wore with pride. Donks Morely was the bookies runner who lived in the top house on Edward Road and stood at the street corner every betting day of the year. I often saw that bloke and wondered what on earth he was doing day in day out stood on the same spot stamping his feet to keep warm in the freezing cold! Jim Barrouclough, who lived on Coleridge Road/ Kingslake Street, was a bloke who wasn't well when he came home after the war. He would march up and down the road in an army greatcoat sometimes looking in dustbins and he'd always sit on the coursey edge and cobble his shoes. Poor man – he painted the words 'Welcome Home Tom' above his front door but his brother never came home – he died in Burma. He lived with his aged parents whose home I have been told was absolutely spotless.

Another great character from yesteryear was Freddie Thornhill who walked the streets with his horse and cart selling his vegetables. Freddie would shout 'Carrotts, carrots 2d a pound, carrots as big as your mesters!' (Really Fred) I used to go to his yard and stables on Amberley Road on a Sunday morning to get the potatoes for Sunday dinner. He looked like a farmer, always wore a nick hat, waistcoat and wellies. I have heard he used to sit in the front row at The Palace when the Tiller Girls were on with a ten-bob note hanging out his top pocket. I wonder what that signified?

Top: Frank with grandparents Bill Frost and Ada Frost nee Cooper in 1949. Frank age five here, says this photo was taken by Fred Nagg, (you couldn't make a name like that up could you?) A professional photographer he came round the streets knocking on doors. Frank says Gran couldn't resist and was always having them took.

Right: A sight most of us were familiar with Gran'ma Ada always outside either on a chair or sitting on the doorstep watching the world go by. With her in this picture is her married daughter Rosie O'Conell and Rosie's daughter Betty at their front door.

Carbrook Kids 1951-1956

Like all kids who lived on The Common in the 1950's there was always something to do after school and somewhere to go. No one stayed in. There was the Brownies, Guides, Girls' Life Brigade, play centre and Sunday school. When you weren't attending any of these there was the Rec to play in. Carol Cowles of Ravenscarr Road recalls going to the Junior Life Brigade at one chapel and Sunday school at another although they were C. of E. It was the same with all of us, who ever was offering a free cup of tea and a bun we'd be there! Carol and her family got an exchange in 1953 with a family on Manor Park but went back to the area frequently because her grandmother still lived there.

In the first photo taken in Carol's back yard we have on the front row left to right; Carol Cowles, Angela Rhodes and Marylin Davitt. On the back row left to right are: Joan Rudkin, Barbara Buxton and Linda Rhodes. Carol writes, "Linda was my best friend, I sold my tortoise to her for a penny. The Rhodes family moved to Essex and we lost contact but she was visiting relatives around the time I was getting married and she must have got my address from my grandma and she came to the wedding. She was most likely visiting her cousin June Loomes who lived in the top yard cornering Carltonville Road. Barbara Buxton went on to the City Grammar School and I met up with her again there. I had moved to the Manor Park Estate when I was eight and went of Pipworth Road School. Another girl I knew there from Carbrook was Myra Damms."

The Coronation Party held at Carbrook Conservative Club 1953. Carol Cowles in seated on the front table next to the wistful lad in N.H.S. glasses. On the other side of her is Geoffrey Bamber whom Carol seems to think lived on Howden Road. The gentleman in the front is the man who had the herbalist shop. Now was that the one bang opposite Carltonville Road? The one with the juke box by the window or was it the herbalist shop just past the Pavilion? The girl next to him looks remarkably like Linda Barnes. I have been told the wistful lad is Michael Schofield who lived on Bold Street and the lad on the left Malcolm Spalding off Edward Road.

This photo records **The Crowning of The May Queen 1951** at the **United Methodist Church Clifton Street**. The girl with the crown of flowers on her head is June Loomes - The May Queen. On the front row left is Barbara Furness, then Glynis ?, Carol Cowles holding the basket of petals, ?, Veronica Myers, then slightly back is Marylin Myers and behind her Hilery Cotton who had a brother called Billy. Every year at Whitsuntide the May Queen and her Attendants would be carried on the back of a lorry to Carbrook Rec for the Whit Parade and open air service.

This is the cast of 'Aladdin', which was put on by the **Ebenezer Wesleyan Chapel Sunday School, Surbiton Street** just off Broughton Lane c. 1956. Sunday School member Veronica White who lived on Howden Road, a fair distance, says the elders at this church were so friendly and welcoming it was worth the walk. Some of the kids in the picture are Mary Harris, Anne White, Jean Walker, Veronica White, Susan Walker and Doreen Burke and they are all in a group left of centre as you look at the photo.

Ted Fairbanks & The Deighton Garage on Old Hall Road

Ted Fairbanks who lived on Abinger Street just over the bridge on top Coleridge worked at this garage from leaving school and says there was a very nasty accident here in the early 50's. On the left of the photo is the wall that held up the scrap yard at Brown Bayley's. There used to be a curtain made from iron chains hanging down. This stopped the great pile of scrap metal from shifting and falling over the wall. Moving the scrap around was a giant crane and one day it toppled over and came crashing down into the road. I can't remember if Ted says it actually hit the garage or not. Working in the great Steel Works was not only dangerous for the workforce itself but also for the folk who lived in the neighbouring streets.

Outside the garage doors of the Deighton Motor Company are, left to right:-

Ronald Dixon, Arthur Dixon, Ted Fairbanks and Gordon Mellor. At the back is Malcolm Foster.

This photo was taken around 1950/51

Postcards Past & Present

"BEAUTIFUL SHEFFIELD"

H 1045

As others saw us

As it really was

VIEWS OF THE STREETS SHOPS AND PLACES WE ONCE KNEW

Belmoor Road 1953

A rarely seen view of the very top end of Belmoor Road where it met with Manningham Road. This was before the East Forge extension began in 1957 with the erection of buildings and plant for the production of forgings rings and railway tyres. Terry Green used to work in the East Forge in the 1950's. Terry came off Attercliffe Common near Clifton Street and I blame him for all the racket that went on morning noon and night when I was growing up there!

Just look how clean and tidy this road was, with no signs of litter or graffiti on the walls. And look how well dressed are all the windows with their sills clean and well polished with red cardinal and the steps with white cardinal. If you couldn't afford that then donkey stone would have to do. This was got from the rag-man in exchange for a bundle of old clothes.

The folk living at the very top of Belmoor Road in 1953 were:-

80	Violet Gregg
78	Tom Merchant
76	Tom & Annie Handley, Alfred Pickersgill,
	Fred & Kath Merchant
74	Ruby & Ernest Bradley
72	James & Ann Smith
70	Webster
68	Albert & Sarah Circuit
66	Kenneth & Irene Duffey

During the war children were taken out of Carbrook County School and taught in the front rooms of the homes on the right of the frame, though it looks as if they are empty now. On this run of shops was an undertaker's and as kids we used to dare one another to knock on the front door of the shop and shout 'Have you got any empty boxes?' The shop set back was Dobson's household goods and drapery. It was originally a doctor's surgery and it was there my sister Mavis was carried to when she collapsed in the Rec one day suffering from Rheumatic Fever.

A lorry delivering to Gallons on the left. Beyond, The Cosy Furnishing Co., then Mawsons – Cobblers ending at Carltonville Road. On the first left you can just see part of Shultz Pork Butchers. I used to hear stories about the people who owned this shop who were German, having bricks thrown through their windows every weekend during the First World War. On the right is the top of Janson Street.

My favourite place: the Library on Leeds Road. This is the Children's Dept

A last farewell to some of the original dwellings in Carbrook. Fronting the Common and opposite Lock House Road this run is between Southern Street and Weedon Street. The old Union pub was a flop house in its later years and on the right was Les Fox's Homely Stores. George Banks removed to new premises on Carlisle Street. Just further up near the corner with Warden Street John Goulder who built most of Carbrok had his yard. Goulder Place near Broughton Lane was named after him and his brothers.

Collin's Rag Yard – Edward Road

This was Collin's Rag and Scrap Yard with its entrance on Edward Road. This photo looks as if it was taken from the back bedroom of Mrs Allsop's house on Amberley Road. Doesn't it look dire! My granddad was a steelworks carter and he had his own horse and cart. When he was out of work he did a bit of rag collecting and kept his cart and horse stabled here. The Old Attercliffe Pottery was sited here with its clay pits just further up towards Manningham. My younger brother Martin says he remembers seeing small clay pots on shelves here. They were probably items left over when the Old Pottery closed in the 1870's. Would you believe our Roger used to pinch my clothes then take them to the yard and get them weighed in for pocket

money! Look closely at the bedroom window on the extreme left. Is that a face at the window – if so then it's Wendy Bloom.

I would guess it was the Health Inspectors who took this picture as a just argument for its demolition.

Back yards in the middle of a Lump somewhere on The Common.

CASTLETON WHITSUNTIDE 1955.

Front Row:- Geoffrey Levesley, Barbara Burditt, Sylvia Yeardly ?, ? Lightowler, Beverley Dewhurst, Michael Sheldon, Grant Froggatt.

We were in the first year when this photo was taken. I was in J1A and our teacher was Miss Gillott. I remember the trip but not the photo. We went into the big cave at Castleton, the one where there's a stream running through it and I remember the guide pleading with us not to push the rock into the water as he was fed up of pulling it out every week. The girls twigged on straight away but all the boys gave it a shove, as if it would move, it was the size of a bus! The only other trip I remember was the one to London. This was for the fourth year but as there were some places to fill they went round J3A & B. We set off about 7.00 a.m. getting on the coach at Terry Street to the station to get The Master Cutler. As ever I was sick all the way there and back. Enjoyed London though. I remember going with Christine Grayson because we both went to the Slipper Baths the day before and we actually had the nerve to ask the bath attendant if we could have some more hot water put in the bath! (All taps were operated outside the bath cubicles and strictly rationed.)

Blaco Road in 1971.

The road to school and the road to play, this is Blaco Road after Brown, Bayley's moved everyone off our Lump in order to extend the East Forge from the other side of Manninghm Road in 1956. The photographer stood on Amberley Road to get this view and on the left are the tops of Berkley Road and Belmoor Road. Who did the little Dachshund belong to I wonder.

Roger Sapcote at the top of Terry Street 1988. Most of the photos in this book are from his collection.

THE FISHERMAN'S REST – TINSLEY PARK ROAD

If any man said they had been for a drink on Top Common, everyone knew he meant Tinsley Park Road. The fact is Attercliffe Common originally butted up to Darnall Common nearly to Coleford Road, so this is a saying from antiquity. There was a small skittles alley behind this pub.

One last ice cream from Hill Top Dairy 1988.

Next door the Islamabad restaurant occupies the site of one of the first Asian food outlets on the Common. The Ismail Jama dining rooms was opened by a Somali c.1957.

The land by the Labour Exchange was purchased by Gamaliel Milner and Richard Swallow in 1779 for the building of a workhouse.

It was pulled down in 1864 after the Poor Law was passed and its inmates removed to the Kelham Island Workhouse. The Vestry Hall was built on the site.

Roger Sapcote took this superb shot of Carbrook County Junior & Infants School in 1990. I always meant to go inside and have a look before the juniors was demolished but never got round to it. Weren't the old schools well built? And look at the design – breathtakingly beautiful– don't you agree?

Do you see the arch window by the back entrance. Under the window was a large sink and if you were caught with a tide-mark on your arms or neck then you had to wash in cold water. On one occasion a teacher ordered two girls to fully bath one child in that sink in cold water.

The school nurse used to call regularly and held court in the first room on the ground floor corridor. She would weigh you and look at your body, (was she looking for signs of mal treatment?) and then look through your hair. There was usually one child per class who got the dreaded letter informing their mothers that they had an infestation of the head.

My brother Brian recalls the school motto painted on the wall in the hall, **BE A ROWER NOT A DRIFTER**.

Another memory from the 1950's comes from Leslie Walker who lived on Goulder Place who said Miss Denman used to ask George White not to come to school in clogs as nobody could hold a conversation whenever he walked across the wooden parquet floor.

A SAD FAREWELL – CARBROOK BOARD SCHOOL BUILT 1889

What insanity to order the demolition of our fine school and Newhall Road School (1873), the first in the country to be built as a result of Forster's Education Act of 1870. So much of our heritage has been lost by the crass indifference of those who were supposed to care for it.

In the 1950s the B.B.C. used to broadcast schools' programmes and one such was the music and dance lesson that was held in the upstairs hall. Listen, can you hear the children singing?

Girls: "Brother come and dance with me, both my hands I offer thee,

right foot first, left foot then, round about and back again."

Boys: "I would dance but don't know how, when to jump or when to bow,

show me what I ought to do, so that I may dance like you.

Girls: "With your feet you tap, tap, tap. With your hands you clap, clap, clap.

Right foot first, left foot then round about and back again"
(from Hansel & Gretel)

The corner of **Goulder Place** and Attercliffe Common with Syd Smith's Bike shop and further up was James' Cycle Shop, a favourite haunt of all my sons who would push their broken bikes up Janson Street then ride home all fixed but with me a few quid lighter.

This run of shops was between Milford Street and Carbrook Street and as part of Carbrook Terrace was built in 1854.

Talk about letting the side down! They haven't seen a paintbrush since the day they were put up. The plus side though is it gives those of us interested in early Victorian properties a chance to see some original windows.

ALLTOOLS removed from the top of Carbrook Street to the old Broughton premises. Weren't Victorian pubs attractive buildings? Like the cinemas they offered refuge and escape from a world over which the working man and woman had no control.

The Silver stream that once was Bradley Nook Road. Now Coleridge Road and named after the first M.P. for Attercliffe in 1887. Now at the death, but still recognisable, are the street corners where lived old friends and neighbours. On the left at the junction with Manningham, the home of Philip Wade and on the corner facing was Tom Kirby's shop and behind that the home of Frank Sutcliffe, his aunt Rose and his Grandma Ada. On the right you can just make out the junction of Kingslake Street where Mr Gethin had his fruit & veg shop.

Coleridge Road with Glave Street and Swan Street on the left. The shops facing are Kircups (paint & ironmongers) the double fronted greengrocers and Nur Bros. This was originally a butcher's shop that had a small slaughter- house at the rear. This run of shops was built in 1876.

Attercliffe Sale & Exchange, the Arab café and Ernest B. Giles optician demolished August 1988.

The Roller Skates on the corner of Church Lane and Zion Lane. A corridor was marked out for beginners – Mug's Alley.

Webster's Walk Round Store was on the ground floor. They sold second hand furniture.

The most popular pub on The Common, The Old Gate was lost forever on 8/8/1988.

God Bless her and all who sailed in her.

These two shops are part of The Lambpool block built in 1870 and look as if they are stone built but the pub itself has been rendered. Taken in the winter of 62/63 and it's siling down. The cottages on the right are the new ones marked out on the O.S. map of 1851. Note the fashion styles in windows.

Attercliffe Common with the corner of Whitworth Lane. Hartley's Drapers is where mother took us to buy clothing and underwear which was kept in cardboard boxes and stacked on shelves. Never went in the shops on either side, the swap shop and the barber's shop. They were men's shops! Likewise you never saw a man in Abbotts – Ye Olde Wool Shop – just past Terry's Dining Rooms. That was the shop where women got their requisites on their Lady Days which were wrapped in brown paper and handled as if they were contraband. Miss Abbott would die if she saw the ads. on T.V. today!

This run of shops was know as the Newbould Buildings and was erected in 1875, five years after The Salutaion and surrounding homes were built. The gap to the right led to court no.6 Attercliffe Common and originally there were two more shops beside The Old Gate. In my day the run of shops here was:- Buckleys (Minnies)- Stationery, toys, 2d Library (o.k. if you liked Zane Gray Westerns). Garretts -Fruit & Veg. Platts Sweets, Almey- grocer, Thorpe-Butcher, Second Hand Shop, Robins-Ladies Hairdresser, Hartley-Herbalist, Florist, Dry Cleaners, Fane-Glass & Pottery, Gethin & Wainwright-Doctor's Surgery, Sandwich Shop, The Gate, Brayshaws-Toy, Dolls Hospital & Newsagent, Bread Shop, Chip Shop.

The old Salutation bereft of its yellow tile cladding and the old café. Not sure of their place in the scheme of things they were finally removed in time for the world student games so they wouldn't show the place up!

راجہ برادرز کی دوکان ہل ٹاپ کی قبرستان کے سامنے

Raja Bros shop was situated between the Doctor's Surgery and the Pavilion Cinema. It was established in 1967 and was the biggest and most successful of the Asian shops.   Raja Sahib traded here for 20 years before moving to Staniforth Road.   This photo was taken just before its demolition in 1990.   In the 1950's there was a Herbalist's shop here.   As kids we used to fetch herbs for our parents and have a glass of Vimto while the order was being made up.

راجہ برادرز کی دوکان پادلین سنیما اور ڈاکٹر کی سرجری کے درمیان میں واقع تھی 1967ء میں قائم کی گئی تھی
اور ساری پاکستانی دوکانوں میں سب سے بڑی اور سب سے کامیاب تھی۔ راجہ صاحب یہاں پچپیس سال تک کاروبار
کرتے رہے اس کے بعد سٹانیفور تھ روڈ پر منتقل ہو گئے۔ یہ فوٹو دوکان گرنے سے تھوڑی دیر پہلے 1990ء میں کھنچا تھا۔
1950'sء میں یہ جڑی بوٹیوں کی دوکان ہوتی تھی ،ہم بچپن میں اپنے والدین کے لیئے دوا لینے آتے تھے اور جب تک
دوکاں دار دوا تیار کرتا تو ہم بچے اس کے انتظار کے دوران مشروب وِمٹو (vimto) سے لطف اندوز ہوتے تھے۔

Old Hall Road and Whitworth Lane in 1988

Old Hall Road in the foreground with Whitworth Lane to the right and Howden Road to the left. The old police station built in the 1870s is still in use and waiting for the new building fronting the Common to be completed. The Vestry Hall and old Labour Exchange (white Building) are on the top left.

The Deighton Motor Company's showroom on Old Hall Road, with its quasi Art Deco frontage. Holbeck Street and Baildon Street are still visible in the background. The run of shops above are the backs of The Newbould Buildings with The Old Gate at the side of the gap. Still dominating the scene is the works on Hawke Street. Was that the old Gun Shop, built tall so gun barrels could be hoisted up on cranes without hitting the roof?

**AND QUIET FLOWS THE DON – THE WEIR HEAD BY CARBROOK STREET.
THERE HAS   BEEN A WEIR ON THIS SITE SINCE 1328.**

**OVER THE BRIDGE. WHAT A WEALTH OF STORIES THE GOOD FOLK OF
TOP COMMON AND DARNALL HAVE TO TELL OF LIFE THERE IN THE 50'S & 60'S.**

**PART OF THE LAST REMAINING SECTION OF THE PUMP POND
TINSLEY PARK WOODS 2003**

THESE SYLVAN SCENES ARE OF THE JESUS CHAPEL AND HILL TOP CEMETERY BUILT IN 1629 – "THAT EVER FIXÉD MARK"

A view down Oakes Green to St. Charles Street.

This is where Uncle Joe, Aunt Gladys and twin cousins Joe and Tony Sapcote lived.

We think these cheeky lads are somewhere off Leigh Street. 1962. (or was it Staniforth Road?)

Here again we have streets that are clean and free from the modern scourge of graffiti and litter.

A family on Newark Street in 1962.

Bibliography

A History of Old Attercliffe	G.R. Vine
Schools in an Urban Community	Cheryl Wing Parsons
Yorkshire Pots & Potteries	H.Lawrence
Evidence on the Employment of Children	J.C.Symonds
We'll Be Masters Now	Dr. J.Baxter
Workers Housing in West Yorkshire	Hobson
A Pub on Every Corner	D. Lamb
The Illustrated Guide to Sheffield 1862	Pawson & Brailford
Street Names of Sheffield	Peter Harvey
Radio Comedy 1938-1968	Foster & Furst
Electoral Registers 1952-1967	Sheffield City Libraries

Leaflets, Almanacks, Newspapers.
A Catalogue of Ancient Charters…. Compiled by T. Walter Hall (Via Mrs Hilda Lowe, English Mistress, Coleridge Girls' School 1959.)
Survey of the Parish of Sheffield – Township Of Attercliffe-cum-Darnall,
The Church in Attercliffe,
Attercliffe Parish Magazine May 1957 Vol.4, No. 5
Whitackers Attercliffe Almanack 1880,
Transcripts of Baptismal Records at Attercliffe Chapel 1720-1811
Sheffield & Rotherham Independent 16.6.1896.
Brown, Bayley Newsletter 1972
Darnall O.S.1903 Map Notes by T. Lodge

Acknowledgements

I would like to thank the following people who have helped me with my research, made contributions to the book and for help in improvement of phrase and construction and for keeping me in stitches while regaling stories from Attercliffe's past, including those which for decency's sake could not be printed. My thanks nonetheless to: Elaine Morgan, Bert Tranter, Moreen Perry, Barry Walker, Jane Leversidge, Brenda Melia, Ann Robinson, Dr. Joanna Cannon, Arthur Liddell, Joan and Audrey Outram, Janis Brooks, The Hillery Family, Leslie Walker, Sandra Brownhill, Linda Kelford, Terry Hibberson, The Rev. John and Mrs Phillada Ware, Frank Sutcliffe, Veronica White, Carol Cooper, Frank Sutcliffe, Ted Fairbanks, David Ainscough and Dr John Baxter. And to any I have omitted without intention.

I would also like to record my appreciation for all the material that was made available to me by all the staff at Local Studies Library, Surrey Street, Sheffield.

To Roger Sapcote for his photographs, technical information, advice and encouragement.

To Mrs Isidore Lewis for gifting the Brownie Box Camera to our mother in 1951 which enabled her to record our childhood days in Attercliffe.

And lastly, I would like to award a posthumous knighthood to the late G.R.Vine, Head Master of Huntsman's Gardens 1906-1932 for his services to local history in Attercliffe.

APPENDIX

Swan Street 1958
Odd Numbers
No 1 FOTHERGILL- Charles, Ruth.
No 3 BRAMMAN – George, Doreen.
No 5 TAYLOR- Frank, Joan.
No 7 HOLMES – James, Elizabeth.
No 9 GRAY- James, Emily.
No 11 WOODHEAD- Ada, Tom.
       BURTON Frank.
No 13 SPYE- Charles, Mona.
No 15 WRIGHT- Adelaide
No 17 LONGDEN – Herbert, Selina
No 19 PEAKER – Evelyn, Harold.
No 21 THOMPSON – Arthur, Annie.
No 23 BARRETT – William, Gladys.
No 25 SLACK – Beatrice, Edith.
No 27 BUFFEY – Ernest, Lily.
No 29 DICKINSON – Martha.
No 31 HANCOCK – Raymond, Joan.
Court Number one/ Swan Square
1/1 PULLEN – George, Sylvia.
1/2 GRAYSON – Betsy
1/3 SMITH – Charles.
1/5 CLAXTON – Colin.
1/6 JONES – Frederick, Emma.
1/7 SLACK – John, Lucy
1/8 HENSON – Albert, Edna.
No 33 ENEFEY, Ernest, Edna.
No 35 BARRETT – George, Ada.
No 37 WILKINSON – Herbert, Mary.
No 39 PARTRIDGE – Edwin, Elizabeth.
No 41 MINNIS – Alexander, Jane, Leonard.
       ROBINSON – Hannah.
No 51 GREEN – William, Mary.
No 53 BAXTER – George, Lena.
Even Numbers
No 2 NICHOLS- William, Louisa.
No 4 SKELTON – Gerald, Ida.
No 6 BECKINGHAM – Drucilla.
No 8 SMITH – Florence.
No 10 BOYT – Fred, Mary.
No 14 ATCLIFFE – Ernest.
No 18 CHAMBERS – Fred.
No 20 HOWDEN – Frank, Eileen.
No 22 LONGDEN – William, Marjorie.
No 24 APPLEBY – George, Nellie.
No 28 GREEN – John, Sally.
No 30 ROBINSON – Ernest, Annie. KELLY – Alice.
No 32 BIRKINSHAW – Alfred, Ivy.
No 34 MILLINGTON – Florrie.
No 36 HANCOX – Lilian, Sydney.
No 38 ANTHONY – William, Ann.
       OSBORNE – Albert, Edith.
No 40 BEAZLEY – Emma.
No 42 SCREATON – Charles, Alice.
No 44 GILL – Benjamin. FURNESS – Fred, Esther.
No 46 WOODS – Mary, Dennis.
No 48 WHITAM – Ernest, Lily.
No 50 STRINGER – Joseph, Clara.
No 52 GREEN – George, Kathleen.
No 54 NOBLE – Wilfred, Mary.

Manningham Road 1952
Odd Numbers
No 1 RICHARDS – Florence, John.
No 3 STOKES – Joseph.
       SMITH – Lily, Arthur.
No 5 QUEEN – Elsie.
No 7 TIMMS – Fred, Ethel.
No 9 YOUNG – George, Kate, George jnr.
No 11 HARRISON – Ethel, Robert.
No 13 ROWBOTHAM – David, Elizabeth.
No 15 HILLERY – Elsie, William.
No 17 SAPCOTE – George, Gladys J.
No 19 DUNN – Tom, Ellen.

No 21 no entry
No 23 OUTRAM – Eric, Lily.
No 25 SLACK – Richard, Gert. Jean.
No 27 BINGHAM – John, Florence, Stephen
No 29 PITTS – Frank, Doris.
No 31 SLACK – John, Violet.
       RISKEY – Oliver, Alice.
No 33 RHODES – William, Nellie.
No 35 SCARROTT – Richard, Sarah, Lucy.
No 37 NOBLE – Wilfred, Mary.
No 39 GRAYSON – William, Mary.
No 41 GRAYSON – Charles, Evelyn.
No 43 BRADLEY – Jessie, Charles.
No 45 HAILES – Alice, Roy.
No 47 POINTER – Stephen, Ann.
No 49 STANDISH – Willie, Lily.
No 51 HUTCHINSON- Harry.
       DAVIS – Joseph, Annie.
No 53 CIRCUIT – Gwen, Alfred.
No 55 SAVAGE – Arthur, Lucy.
No 57 no entry
No 59 no entry
No 61 O'BRIEN – William, Doris.
No 63 BELL – Seth, Flora.
No 65 WHITHAM – Wilfred, Rose.
       WHITHAM – Eric, Freda.
No 67 MATSON – Amelia.
No 69 BURNHAM – Annie.
       GRAYSON – Ida, Isaac,
No 71 CLARKSON – Ida, Ben.
No 73 BRADLEY – Florence, Arnold, William.

Blaco Road 1954
Even numbers
No 2 FELKIN – John. YOUNG, Lily, Leslie.
No 4 JACQUES – Lydia, Margaret.
       WHEELER – Victor, Annie.
No 6 DAVITT – John, Renee.
No 8 TAYLOR – Nora, Edwin.
No 10 JONES – Mary, Frank.
       BRAY – John, John jnr.
No 12 GRAHAM – Jean, Denton.
No 14 COLK – Ethel, Joseph.
No 16 FOX – John, Martha.
No 18 MARSH – Walter, Laura.
No 20 MARSH – Fred, Jean.
No 22 RICHARDSON – Jonathan.
No 24 PORTER – Mary.
No 26 HAMMOND – Bertha, Marjorie.
       WHITEHOUSE – Gladys, Oliver.
No 28 KNIGHT – Ellen.
No 30 BUXTON – Beatrice, Walter.
No 32 WESTWOOD – Nora, Thomas.
No 34 HARRISON – Annie.
No 46 GELSTHORPE – George.
No 48 SOCKETT -Betty, Sydney.
No 50 SIMPSON – Colin, Jean.
No 52 SMITH – Sheila, Annie, John, Edith.
No 54 RHODES – Maud, George.
No 56 ROBERTSON – Roy, George, Edith.
No 58 MOFFATT – James.
Odd Numbers
No 1 BEAUMONT – Albert, Hannah. RASON – Hannah, William.
No 5 ALLSOP – Ada, Fred.
No 11 BROWN – Kathleen. MORRIS – Emma, Wallace.
No 23 HOWE – Hilda, George.
No 25 HECTOR – Percy, Leonard.
No 27 DENTON – Martha, James.
No 29 WILSON – Joseph.
No 31 BOTRILL – Margaret, Beatrice, George.
No 33 BRADLEY – Eliza, Joseph.
No35 ALLSOP – Winifred, Edwin.
No 37 WOOD – Louie, David.

Amberley Road 1957

Even numbers

No 2	JENKINSON – George, Mary
No 4	DICKINSON – George, Sarah
No 6	DOBSON – Walter, Lily
No 8	OGLESBY – John
	JONES – Frederick, Margaret
No 10	MITCHELL – James, Frederick. GUESS – Ada, Joseph.
No 12	FRETWELL – Margaret, Walter
No 14	HAGLINTON – Thomas, Evelyn
No 24	BURNHAM – Maud. RUTHAVEN – C. B.
No 28	BURNHAM – Gordon, Dorothy
No 30	HUTCHINSON – Margaret, Stanley
No 32	MORTLEDGE – Rose
No 34	FOWLER – Mary A.
	PALMER – Sydney, Sarah
No36	TAYLOR – Ernest, Ada, Harry
No 40	HAMILTON – Violet, Frederick
	EDWARDS – John, Frank
No 42	PYE – Isaac, Nellie.
	WINGFIELD – Annie, William
No 44	BROWN – Frank.
	LEMON – Charles, Lucy
No 46	HEATON – Brenda, Dennis.
	SULLIVAN – Walter, Hilda
No 50	HIRST – Lizzie, Norman
No 52	NEEDHAM – Lily
No 56	THORNHILL – Frederick, Edith, Fred jnr. Marjorie
No 58	KELLY – Robert, Caroline
No 60	HAGUE – Albert, Mary, Mabel
No 62	GAMBON – George, Christine, Derrick
No 64	ROBINSON – William, Beatrice, Derrick
No 66	HOPEWELL – Dennis. BAILEY – Elizabeth
No 68	GREGG – Harold, Freda
No 70	SWEETING – George. BOOTH – Ruth, Walter
No 72	WILLIAMS – Phyllis
No 74	COLLEY – Herbert, Annie
No 76	BAKER – William, Ellen, Will jnr.
No 78	ALLSOPP – Robert, Joyce
No 80	PILLEY – Harry, Lilly
No 82	PULLEN – Jemima, Walter.
	KNIGHT – Harold
No 84	WILFORD – Gladys
No 86	ROBINSON – Charles, Lilian
No 88	TURNER – Ivy, William

Odd Numbers 1957

No 19	BREARS – Dennis, Iris
No 21	DRANSFIELD – Edna, William
No 23	WINGFIELD – Eli, Grace
No 25	SAVAGE – Ernest, Annie.
	PARFITT – William
No 27	CHILDS – Annie, John
No 29	BIGGINS – Lawrence, Denise
No 31	NIXON – Edith
No 33	FLEET – Harold, Lily
No 35	DAVIES – Lillian
No 37	TAYLOR – Herbert, Irene
No 39	CHILDS – Sylvia
No 47	EARL – Frank, Mabel
No 49	MARGRIM – Rose, Charles
No 51	COTTON – John, Harry
No 53	HOPKINSON – James, Florence
No 55	MITCHELL – Vernon, Mary
No 57	WILLEY – Hilda, Sydney
No 59	WRIGHT – Alfred, Sarah
No 61	PRICE- James, Mary
No 63	WILLEY – George
No 65	SLACK – Herbert, Gertrude
No 67	GAMBON – John, Margaret
No 69	REED – John, Lily
No 71	PARKIN – Walter, Doreen
No 73	BECK – George, Margaret, Annie

Berkley Street 1966/67

Even numbers

No 8	MOYER – William, Edith
No 10	SMITH – Rita, Geoffrey
No 12	ANDREWS – Ronald, Jean,
	PEARS – Susan
No 14	PERRY – George, Florence
No 16	MELLOR – Monica
	SURTEES – Edith
No 18	WARNER – Victor, Elsie, George
No 20	CARR – John.
	TOMBLING – Sara
No 22	PEARS – Alan, Joan
No 24	HOLLAND – Florence, William
No 26	NELSON – Hilda, Leslie
No 28	BUXTON – Lawrence, Florence
No 30	BRIGHTMORE – Joyce, Stephen, Alice
No 32	GREENFIELD – Constance, Donald
No 34	BELL – Mary, George
No 36	BAKER – Emily, Henry
No 38	MITCHELL – Lily
No 40	COX – George.
	WOOD – Rose
No 42	MITCHELL – Elizabeth, Byron
No 44	RICHARDSON – Dinah, John
No 46	CLOUGH – Emily, John
No 48	SMITH – Nellie, James
No 50	HENSON – Elsie, Thomas
No 52	STEAR – Muriel, John
No 54	SALT – Emily,
	WESTON – Eleanor, Charles
No 56	GODDARD – Lois, George
No 58	PALMER – Mabel, Thomas
No 60	WILLIAMSON – Mary
No 62	HOGAN – Hilda, Sydney
No 64	BRADBURY – Isaac
No 66	WINTER – Jack, Edith
No 68	ROBINSON – Mabel, John
No 72	ASH – Francis
No 74	HANCOCK – Nellie

Odd Numbers 1963

No. 5	MITCHELL – Elsie
No. 7	PALMER – Evelyn
No. 9	WHITE – Edith
No. 11	DENNISON – John, Rose, Dorothy
No. 13	DALTON – Sydney, Ethel
No. 15	LONGHURST – Hedley, Ellen
No. 17	GLAVE – Harry, Florence
No. 19	DOWNES – Edward, Grace
No. 21	MANSELL – William, Clara, Ethel, Francis
No. 23	SCOTT – Harry, Elsie.
	ELLIS – Barry
No. 25	WALKER – Florence
No. 27	PARKER – Cyril, Annie
No. 29	BIDWELL – Brian, Peggy
No. 31	OXLEY – John, Elizabeth
No. 33	SMITH – Allen, Eileen
No. 35	HODGESON – Colin, Leonard, Nan
No. 37	BALL – Albert, Dora
No. 39	WILSON – John, Doreen
No. 41	ENSOR – George, Elsie, Florence
No. 43	BOWSER – William, Annie.
	ISHERWOOD – John
No. 45	YOUNG – Jack Ethel
No. 47	HAYCOCK – Harry, Doris
No. 49	ALLFORD – Frank, Alice, Frank jnr
No. 51	MELLOR – Kathleen
No. 53	LANGLEY – John, Patricia
No. 55	LANGLEY – John, Albert, Martha, Nellie
No. 57	PALMER – Archie
No. 59	SUNDERLAND – Maurice, Jessie
No. 61	LAW – Albert, Connie
No. 63	PADLEY – Wallace, Ada
No. 65	HARRISON – Dennis, Freda
No. 71	FLETCHER – John, Betty
No. 73	HILL – Henrietta, Charles, Eileen

Coleridge Road (Salutation to Bridge) 1957

Even numbers

No. 10   CURRY – Doreen, Patrick
No. 12   NUTALL – Jane, Albert
No. 14   CLAYTON – Clara, Clarence
No. 16   SMITH – Elsie, John
No. 18   FOY – Sylvia,
          Back – HOWELL William, MARSDEN Joseph
No. 20   MARTIN – George, Ethel, Amelia, Thomas
No. 22   PITTS – Frank, Doris, Frank jnr
No. 24   HAMMOND – Lily, David
No. 26   HARDY – Walter, Lily
No. 28   SAPCOTE – George E., Gladys J., George, Brian.
No. 30   MORRIS – Hannah,
          WARD – Stanley
No. 32   McCAGUE – Thomas Sarah
No. 36   NORRISS – Arthur, Doreen.
          WEBSTER – Mary, Mathew
No. 38   ROOKER – Emily, Edward
No. 40   GOOSNEY – Marriot, Violet, Rita, Barbara
No. 42   SMITH – Roy, May.
          MELLORS – Auburn
No. 46   THOMPSON – Dora, Collin
No. 48   FURNESS – Eric, Violet, Alfred
No. 50   CHRISTOPHER – William
No. 52   BURGIN – Henry, Louisa, Gordon, Mavis,
No. 54   O'SULLIVAN – John Joseph, Johannah, Michael, Jane, John
No. 56   GETHIN – Charles, Emily
No. 58   RODDIS – Sam, Ada
No. 60   SKIDMORE – Maurice, Lily
No. 62   FARMER – Annie, Eric, Annie jnr
No. 64   WILKS – Alexander, William, Jack
No. 66   JACKSON – Eric.
          WAINWRIGHT – Elsie, Frederick
No. 68   FOSTER – Florence, Ernest
(up the double entry)
Court 6/1 DIXON – Ernest
          JACQUES – Sam, Sarah, Sam jnr., Daniel
     6/2 MANSELL – Mary, Edward
     6/3 BURDITT – Patricia, Harry
     6/4 PITT – Florence, Jennie
No. 70   CLARKSON – Ben, Ivy
No. 72   LEARY – Maggie, John.
          GREEN – Maria
No. 74   COOPER – Muriel, James.
          BOLDWICK – Beatrice
No. 76   WHITEHEAD – Frank, Irene.
          WELLS – Alice M, Arthur
No. 78   KNOWLES – Hannah, William

Odd numbers

No. 3   POTTER – Florence, Edwin
No. 5   HARE – Lilian, John
No. 7   RICHARDSON – John, Dinah
No. 9   O'BRIEN – Alice, Willie
No. 11   WILES – Lily, Gordon
No. 13   RICHARDS – John, Margaret, John
No. 15   non registered
No. 17   CRAPPER – Beatrice.
          PRESSLEY – Lawrence, Barbara
No. 19   FOSTER – Frank, Annie
No. 21   MORGAN – Viner.
          COXON – Bismark
No. 23   BECK – Florence, Ernest
No. 25   EVERITT – John, Sarah, Ronald, John R.
No. 27   WHITAM – William, Joan
No. 29   MARSDEN – Ethel
No. 31   GREGG – Violet. STANTON – Ernest
No. 33   HOWDEN – William
No. 35   SHAW – Frank, Ada
No. 37   BROCKLEBANK – Arthur, Nellie
No. 39   MARSH – Reuben, Ethel
No. 41   BRACE – William, Dorothy
No. 43   PRESSLEY – John, Edith
No. 45   POWELL – Henry, May
No. 47   GRAYSON – William
No. 49   HUMPHRIES – John, Alice
No. 51   STATON – Richard, Alexandra
No. 53   non registered

No. 55   STAPLES – Lilian, Robert
          PARKER – Hannah
No. 57   BURGIN – Joe, Ivy, Brenda
No. 59   ZANELLIE – Elizabeth, Ernest
No. 61   RIDGE – Jane, Annie
          SHELDON – George, Margaret
No. 63   MILLINGTON – Gladys, George
No. 65   RICHARDS – Henrietta
No. 67   SMITH – Margaret, Herbert
No. 69   SMITH – Harold, Nellie, Nellie jnr
No. 71   LEDGER – Percy, Louisa
No. 73   WADE – George, Mary
No. 75/77 KIRBY – Thomas, Violet
No. 79   FROST – Ada.
          O'CONELL – Rosie.
          MEDLEY – John

Amberley Place 1965

Even numbers

No. 2   HECTOR – Percy, Leonard
No. 4   McLAUGHLIN – James, Margaret
No. 6   WHITHAM – Wilfred
No. 8   DUMPLETON – Minnie, Harold
No.10   O'REILLY – David. O'BRIEN – Kathleen, Patrick
No. 12   GOULDEN – Florence, George
No. 14   MILNES – Richard, Jean
No. 16   KELLY – Robert

Odd numbers

No. 5   STAFFORD – Patrick
No. 7   KNIGHT – Albert
          ROBERTS – Joseph
          WILSON – Herbert
          LEVERICK – Harry
No. 9   WHITTAKER – Mary

Belmoor Road 1965

Even numbers

No. 12   BUXTON – Alice, Walter
No. 14   POOLE – Lily
No. 16   LISTER – Lucy, Arthur
No. 18   SMEDLEY – Betsy, George
No. 20   CIRCUIT – Albert
No. 22   SYKES – Joyce, Leonard
No. 24   BATES – Elizabeth. CARR – Irene
No. 26   HUSSELBE – Eliza
No. 28   SMITH – Tom, Mary
No. 32   OTLEY – Charles, Ronald
No. 34   WHEELER – Lilian
No. 36   GREEN – Dennis, Margorie
No. 38   TAYLOR – Irene
No. 40   BARRETT – Leslie, Lilian
No. 42   OUTRAM – Eric, Lilian
No. 44   LOVELL – Mary
No. 46   HILL – William
No. 48   CUTTS – Betty, Frank
No. 50   BEADSLEY – Averhilda
No. 52   MULLINS – William
No. 56   CUTTS – Edwin
No. 60   SHAW – Dorothy, John
No. 64   BULLEN – Harold, Mary

Odd numbers

No. 13   COTTERILL – Pete, Joan
No. 15   BOND – Alice
No. 17   WILSON – Vernon, Mabel, Lois
No. 19   ASKHAM – George, Ellen
No. 21   TAYLOR – Harvey, Margaret
No. 23   SMITH – Dorothy
No. 25   LICHFIELD – Maud, Olive
No. 27   HIRST – Walter
No. 29   TAYLOR – Harry, Keith, Maureen
No. 31   HOWSAM – Walter, Michael
No. 33   BRAMMER – Horace
No. 35   GUN – Kenneth, Mary
No. 37   HOBSON – Hilda
No. 39   WHITHERLEY – Frank, Alice
No. 41   GRAYSON – Gwendoline L. John W.
No. 43   JAQUES – Brian, Beryl

Berkley Road 1963

Even numbers

No. 4	GELDARD – Alfred, May
No. 6	BATTERSBY – Florence.
	LEVERSIDGE – Emma, Joseph
No. 8	BUNTING – Joseph, Margaret
No. 10	TURTON – Marion, Charles
No. 12	KAXMIERKIEWICZ – Kathleen.
	MARSDEN – Ethel
No. 14	McDONALD – Beatrice, William
No. 16	LEVERSIDGE – Kenneth, Clarice, Charles, Hetty
No. 18	LEVERSIDGE- – Mavis, Charles
No. 20	NORMAN – Ivy, Ernest
No. 22	WESTON – Teresa, William
No. 24	SMITH – John, Gladys
No. 26	McCARTHY – John, Rose
No. 28	TURNER – Ivy, William
No. 30	BOOTH – Florence
No. 32	COLE – Edith
No. 34	HILL – Nellie, Rowland
No. 36	BRINSLEY – George, Connie
No. 38	ALLEN – Ivy, Charles
	PINDER – Edward, Iris
No. 40	COUNT – Ada. BRINSLEY – Albert
No. 42	ALLEN – Florence, Charles
No. 44	LEVESLEY – Irene, Carol
No. 46	THORPE – Charles, Evelyn.
	BARSTOW – Evelyn, Ernest
No. 48	SHELTON – Amy
No. 50	SMITH – Lilian, Fred
No. 52	FELLS – Ruth
No. 54	SHIRT – Edith, James

Odd numbers 1961

No. 13	COX – Miriam, Allan
	BATTERSBY – Leslie, Margaret
No. 15	THOMAS – Oswald, Christine
	HUDSON – Ernest
No. 17	NEWTON – Cyril, Barbara
No. 19	BREARLEY – James, Edna
No. 21	PHILLIPSON – Annie, Ernest
No. 23	STEEL – May, Charles, George
No. 25	BOND – Robert
	HASSALE – Frederick, Mabel
No. 27	BOOTH – Amelia
No. 29	BAINES – Annie, Lewis, Enid
No. 31	MAKIN – Lily.DUNWELL – Gertrude
No. 33	DUNWELL – Amelia, Samuel
No. 35	MARTIN – Minnie
No. 37	MEDLEY – Gladys
No. 39	CLAYTON – Edith
	MAHONEY – John
No. 41	RISBY – Olivia, Alice
No. 43	HOLT – Brenda, John
	MELIA – Nellie
No. 45	BEESON – Thomas, Gladys
No. 47	JACKSON – Ada, Charles
No. 49	DEWICK – Richard, Sarah
No. 51	MOSELEY – Hubert, Florence
No. 53	DUNWELL – Samuel, Lily
No. 55	NAZIM – Din. DEAN – Lilian
No. 57	WALDEN – George, Esther

Edward Road 1957

Even numbers

No. 4	MELLOR – Henry, Hetty, Annie
No. 6	McLAUGHLIN – John, Edith
No. 8	HARDY – Robert, Edith
No.10	DUCKER – Eric, Constance (Midwife) James
No.12	HOBSON – William, Mary, Gilbert, Valerie
No.14	BIRCHALL – James, Sarah, Kenneth, Raymond
No.16	MOULDS – Harold, Edith
No.18	ROUND – Maurice, Marjorie
No.20	FEARNE – Joseph, Ada
No.22	MINCHER – Bernard, Hannah, Bernard jnr., Alan
No.24	INKLES – Joseph, Evelyn
No.26	MINCHER – Ronald, Ruby, Frank
No.28	HOWSAM – George, Violet
No.30	ASKWITH – Veronica, William
No.34	BROWN – Alfred, Minnie
	MLYNEK– Olga, Stanlevik.
No.36	FURNESS – Robert, Ada, Joseph, Cyril
No.38	OUTRAM – Ada, David
No.40	CHRISTIAN – Harold, Joyce, Margaret
No.42	BODDY – Elizabeth
No.44	BODDY – Catherine
No.46	SMITH – Jim, Edith
No.48	FURNISS – Robert, Edith
No.50	FAWCETT – John, Annie
No.52	YEARDLEY – Ernest, Sylvia, Colin
No.54	ASHWORTH – Ernest, Agnes
No.56	HOPEWELL – Cyril, Kathleen
No.58	MORLEY – Walter, Albert, George
No.60	ENEFEY – Ronald, Hilda
No.62	RHODES – Thomas, Emma
No.64	RHODES – Bertie, Dinah
No.66	ROBERTS – Derek, Nellie
No.68	STOKES – George, Nora
No.70	NORFOLK – Colin, Brenda
No.72	LEVERSIDGE – William, Jane.

Odd numbers 1954

No.19	JOW – Albert, Jane
No.21	ROWE – Stuart, Joan
No.23	SPALDING – Brian
	CLAYTON – Joseph, Ruth
No.25	BURGIN – Robert, Patricia
No.27	HOLMES – Albert, Jessie
	FOX – Fred.
	TAYLOR – Dorothy
No.29	WIGGETT – Lucy
No.31	ERNSHAW – Mary
No.33	BAKER – Frank, Bessie
No.35	SMALLWOOD – Samuel, Bridget
No.37	PHILLIPSON – Frederick, Hilda
No.39	LANGSTAFF – Sidney, Violet, George
No.41	SLACK – Herbert, Maggie
No.43	DRIVER – Violet.
	SMITH – George
No.45	VINTER – Harold
No.49	EYRE – Harold, Kate, Arnold
No.51	TAYLOR – John
	DAVIES – William
	COOPER – William
No.53	BLOOM – George, Ethel.
No.55	HORROCKS – Henry, Eva.
	MARTIN – Beatrice.
No.57	HOWE – George, Betsey, Dorothy
	DOUTHWATE – Charles
No.59	HELLAWELL – Harold, Lily
	GIBSON – Desmond
	LOWE – Mavis
No.61	HINDLEY – William, Gladys
No.63	SCOTT – Arthur, Elizabeth, Maurice

Attercliffe – Too good to forget!